ENDEAVOR OF HONOR

Anne Bland

AmErica House
Baltimore

© 2001 by Anne Bland.

Although this is a true story, many names have been changed as it is not the author's intention to cause anyone embarrassment.

First printing

ISBN: 1-58851-249-5
PUBLISHED BY AMERICA HOUSE BOOK PUBLISHERS
www.publishamerica.com
Baltimore

Printed in the United States of America

I dedicate this book to my children.

ACKNOWLEDGEMENTS

I wish to pay tribute to my friend, Joan Freeman. She has been a source of great blessing and encouragement. Her patience, humor and hard work, beyond price in the preparation of this book. I can only say "Thank you".

I also want to thank all my family for their loving support and practical contribution to this work.

ENDEAVOR OF HONOR

Foreword
By Mary Stewart Van Leeuwen

In the summer of 1989 I did what many college and university professors do: I responded to a request to teach summer school at an institution other than my own. This particular summer took me to Regent College in Vancouver, British Columbia to teach psychology to a mixed class of lay Christians and seminarians training for ministry. The details regarding my class and my students have since faded into pleasant blur (Vancouver and the west coast of Canada being anything but a hardship posting in the summer), but one incident stands out in my memory quite vividly. Sitting in my office one afternoon preparing my lecture for the next day, with door and windows open for the breeze, I suddenly heard a most unscholarly scuffle of large and small feet proceeding down the hall. Looking up, I saw framed in the doorway of my office a large, bearded bear-like man in his thirties with a toddler in his arms and two children not much older hugging his sides.

"You're Mary Stewart Van Leeuwen, aren't you?" He began without preamble. "I need to talk to you. I'd like you to come and have dinner with my family and me. My name is Flynn Ritchie, and I became a Christian at Yieldingtree Farm in Zambia, just like you." Despite my surprise and puzzlement over how he had accessed my conversion history (he had, it turned out, seen one of my books which I had dedicated to the Blands of Yieldingtree Farm), there was never any question that I would accept his invitation. For as readers will discover in reading Anne Bland's book, Yieldingtree Farm was a place uniquely touched by the Holy Spirit for the extraordinary mix of people-varying by age, sex, education and national origin-who passed through its ever open gates. Its ministry of some twenty years, from the early 1960's to the early 1980's is a testimony to the creative ways in which God can pursue those He has chosen for Himself.

Those two decades, as the reader will be reminded throughout the book, were ones of great political and economic ferment in sub-Saharan Africa. In 1965, when I first went as a Canadian volunteer to teach high school in Zambia, the country was celebrating its first year of independence, the price of its copper was high, and Zambia was jokingly referred to as the "the richest pauper in Central Africa." When I returned in 1970 to collect data for my doctoral thesis in social psychology (the same year that I met Anne and Gordon Bland), students' pre-independence revolutionary spirit had quieted, the economy was still stable, and the University of Zambia had opened its doors to provide me with a research base. The national mood was upbeat, both in Zambia and elsewhere in Africa, and 1965 through 1975 was consequently a decade during which many European and American young people (and even some not so young) came to the continent to spend weeks, months, or occasionally years in search of adventure, in the idealistic pursuit of service, or more often than many of them would admit, in search of their souls.

Coming from North America, with its history of acrimonious tension between anti-intellectual fundamentalists and post orthodox liberals, I had come to thoroughly dislike the human centered theology of the liberal churches in which I had been raised, and had concluded I could not become an Evangelical Christian without putting my mind in permanent cold storage. I discovered how wrong I was when I began visiting the Bland's farm, between rounds of data gathering in Lusaka and elsewhere. Here was a place where, despite modest levels of formal education, God was worshipped with their minds as well as their hearts and the beauty and complexity of God's creation was deeply appreciated. Moreover, they practiced in their extended family life a kind of healing hospitality, which was at once an affirmation of the created goodness of ordinary life and a dim foreshadowing of the great banquet of the Lamb pictured in the Book of Revelation. It was a place quietly saturated in prayer for each person who passed through, and at the same time unpretentiously immersed in practicalities of raising farm stock and developing a part of the property as a conference site. Its atmosphere of spiritual nurture, combined with the invitation to help run a farm in the ruggedly beautiful Central African bush, was just what many of its visitors, myself among them, needed to bring them face to face with the Christ of both creation and redemption.

As "Endeavor of Honor" also describes, the second half of the 1970's was a time of much greater uncertainty in the countries of Central Africa. Not only was there the spill over to Zambia of the independence struggle of what was later to be Zimbabwe (the former Southern Rhodesia), there were also the problems of falling copper prices in Zambia, rising oil prices everywhere, mounting foreign debt and internal political corruption in countries less than perfectly prepared for democratic nationhood. Yet despite - or perhaps because of - these accumulating "dangers, toils and snares," the church in Zambia and its neighboring countries grew, not just institutionally, but by means of creative and dedicated small outreaches such as that exemplified by Yieldingtree Farm. The ministry of its hospitality is a testimony to what God can accomplish when one couple clings to His vision of a unique ministry despite often uncertain financial resources and many spiritual, political and psychological challenges. All of us have God's treasure in earthen vessels, and all of us live brokenly and imperfectly in this time of "the already, but the not yet." God in His mercy separates the gold from the dross of our efforts, and His Kingdom thus continues to grow. That was the case also at Yieldingtree, and may yet be again as a younger generation of Blands has returned to work the farm.

All of this was confirmed as I shared my dinner in Vancouver with another graduate of Yieldingtree farm, I had never met until then. There was much about our subsequent histories that was uncannily parallel: both adult converts to the faith, we had both married "cradle Christians" -- he the daughter of American missionaries to Japan, I the son of Dutch Calvinist immigrants to California. Both of us had been entered specialized Christian vocations -- he as Editor of an urban Christian newspaper, I as a professor in a Christian college setting. Both of us were active leaders in our respective churches, with all the passion and grumbling that inevitably accompanies such a commitment. Both of had been educated in the vocation of parenthood and prayed daily for the spiritual growth of our children. Each of us was, and is, a simple gatekeeper in the house of the Lord. But take this and multiply it by the hundreds who passed through Yieldingtree Farm, and the Kingdom of God is much enriched as a result. Anne Bland's account of that ministry will give a glimpse into God's on going narrative of redemption in one corner of the world and is one that will richly repay any reader's attention. **

Endeavor of Honor

"If I rise on the wings of the dawn, if I settle on the far side of the sea, even there your hand will guard me, your right hand will hold me fast."

–Psalms 139: v 9-10

All Scripture references are quoted from the New International Version.

PART 1

1956-1979

Chapter 1
The Builder's Daughter

Inky blackness threw pale reflections of my face back through my window as the train thundered toward a destiny I could only guess at and a meeting for which I had waited five long months.

The previous week had been a heady mix of emotions and exhilaration as I embraced new experiences, having said farewell to my family, crossed the Atlantic to Halifax in Nova Scotia and boarded the train that would take me to the prairies of Saskatchewan.

Brilliant sunshine greeted me next morning, bouncing off an endless white landscape, an ever moving vista of frozen land, trees and lakes. It was a three-day journey. How is it, I thought, that I had already come so far yet felt my journey was barely beginning? It seemed to me then that it was a lifetime since I had stood on the canal bridge near my home in England, longing and praying for something to change. But it had been only little more than three years since that day.

* * *

An unexpected gust of wind blew my long hair across my face and snatched at my hair ribbon. My hand was too slow to catch it, and from the bridge I watched the strip of blue silk float down to the dark water below among a scattering of autumn leaves. For a moment I lingered, reluctant to return to the stifling monotony of my office, which was built alongside our family home only a few steps away.

Overhead an aircraft roared into the sky from the airport a mile away. My eyes followed it out of sight, and I sighed as I turned away. Would it ever be my turn? The summer was over and the winter loomed. Would it be better next year?

Despite a good education to age 16, I had not been encouraged to go on with my education nor seek any other employment. My father insisted I come into the family business, which had been father-to-son for more than a hundred years. My brother John, three years younger, still had to finish school and do his National Military Service. With the pressures of failing health and financial difficulties built up during the war years, my father was adamant. Two efforts to strike out on my own for another job ended in humiliation and defeat. Without training it was extremely difficult and family pressure hard to resist.

My brother left school and joined a man's world. While waiting to do his National Military Service, he began an apprenticeship in the family trade of building construction. His natural aptitude as a craftsman was far stronger than his desire to be involved in management, office work and the like.

But things were about to change for me. An introduction from a mutual friend brought Gordon Bland into my life. He was a young farmer working in Africa, so a pen friendship developed over the next eighteen months.

We shared many interests and it came as a welcome surprise to me that this opportunity to get to know someone whose life was so different could also open the door to meeting other interesting people. Our shared Christian faith made acquaintance even more acceptable. In the midlands of England I was lonely as was he in Nyasaland. From time to time this interest was bolstered by meetings with some of his Christian friends on leave in England or passing through.

The eldest of five children of missionary parents, he was born in Bolivia. The family returned to England and subsequently moved around as his father was appointed vicar of several Anglican Churches. After attending agricultural college, Gordon joined the British Colonial Service and went to Nyasaland, British Central Africa in 1948. Later he moved to Kikuyu Estates to become manager of a group of farms in the same area.

In the early 1950's a group of Canadian missionaries moved into the district. They were looking for somewhere to live while they built their first mission and accepted Gordon's offer of hospitality. Gordon spoke Nyanja, the local language fluently and thereafter spent a lot of time assisting and translating for them in the surrounding villages. Their friendship flourished and in 1957 Gordon decided not to renew his contract with Kikuyu Estates. Instead he would take up his missionary friends' suggestion and enroll in their training college. So it was that he came to England early in that summer with plans to go to Canada the following October.

By this time I had been working in the family business for seven years. There was little opportunity to get out. My brother had commenced his National Service the previous year and my father's health had deteriorated. The business was plagued with financial problems and the resulting stress was hard on us all. While I was a willing assistant to my father, my situation seemed more than ever to be without choice or advantage. From childhood, I had never questioned the presence of God and grew up enchanted by His creation. The most enjoyable times were when I could escape from the monotony of my working week, to go walking for miles in the surrounding countryside. Accompanied by my dog, Patch, I spent the weekends and long summer evenings in the woods and fields.

Through years of attendance at St Nicholas Parish Church, Elmdon and from what my father taught me, I had learned one thing of great value: a consciousness of a loving God, a God who was there. A neighbor, Mrs. Brown, invited me to a Youth for Christ rally in Birmingham Town Hall when I was 17, and there I saw for the first time, the transforming Spirit of God light up a human being and understood enough of that marvelous fusion, the possibility of that most precious relationship between God and individual men. My own conviction of sin and a desire to have that gift drove me to my feet.

Before I left the building that night I had embarked on a new life. Everything I knew and subsequently learned from God's word rang true and I began to think differently. Later when the Browns' 21-year-old daughter died of polio, the situation was something of a milestone for me also, for I saw in the girl's family a depth of faith that was impressive in its strength and peace. My own budding faith was deepened, and the assurance that a fearless future was possible took a firm hold in my life.

After a summer spent mostly together, Gordon and I were married at Elmdon, Warwickshire. We honeymooned at Capernwray Hall in Lancashire. The only thing that cast a cloud over that time was my father continued ill health. It was causing great anxiety. How I longed to go to college and study with Gordon, but I had no savings and only a tiny wage. Our wedding was very modest, and when Gordon had paid for his passage to Canada, his train fare across to Saskatoon and his year's college fees, there was no money left. Indeed he could only afford a cheap passage on some Greek immigrant ship sailing under a 'flag of convenience.' We took the decision that I would stay back and follow in the New Year and hopefully follow Gordon into college the next term. So off he went, while I waved my little damp hanky on the dockside. When the ship was out of sight, I left Southampton to go back home.

But my father's health continued to deteriorate, and we decided Mother should apply to get my brother released from the Army. This request was made on compassionate grounds with the help of the Church Army and was successful, by which time I had managed to get a ticket on the Cunard Liner 'Sylvannia,' which was new and promised me a much more pleasant trip than Gordon's had been. And so in early March I finally set sail.

It was still dark when the train pulled into Saskatoon. An ice cold wind hurtled across the prairies intent on giving me a real arctic welcome, but Gordon was there muffled to his eyebrows in quilted car coat, snow boots and woolly hat and gloves. I was not quite so completely equipped, but the friend who had brought him over a hundred miles to meet the train, whisked me into the warm station restaurant and introduced me to the delights of pancakes dripping with maple syrup and lots of hot coffee. I had arrived, and it was lovely for us to be together again.

Life in a small college town on the Canadian prairies still in the grip of winter proved an exiting experience. Our small basement room introduced me to central heating. That and doing my shopping in supermarket was a revelation. With only two other married couples in the college, who were living out, we tended to visit their modest living quarters quite often. They taught me how to initially cook a one-pot stew on top of a pot bellied wood stove and how to keep it cooking with no further fuel by placing it in a hay box. The hospitality from staff members enabled me to taste for the first time strawberry shortcake, angel food cake 6" deep, potato salad and root beer, while meals taken at the students' canteen introduced me to wienies and sauerkraut.

Whether it was the fault of the lovely rich food or the altitude, or most likely the combination, I suddenly felt so ill, I could hardly stand, nor barely lift my hairbrush for a few days. I was prostrate. Yet in answer to specific prayer, this condition left me as abruptly as it had arrived. As soon as I was up and about again, we had some important decisions to make.

There were a few weeks of term left and then the college would close for the whole summer according to the Canadian system. The students dispersed to earn money for the next years' fees, some to join a church or to go to Summer Camp where they could gain valuable experience. It seemed most students already had plans. We did not, and since we needed a car to get around this vast rural area, we decided I should find a job to get us a little money. We hoped to find direction by the time the college closed.

I found a job at the Town Clerk's Office and happily spent a few weeks typing out utility bills and the like. At lunchtime I took the opportunity to explore the town, to see the dramatic seasonal change that heralded the spring, the arrival of the Chinook. Frozen roads were transformed overnight into seas of glutinous red mud that rolled up on car tires and generally gave a good impression of slimy soft toffee. I believed folk when they told me this earth grew terrific grain.

One of the things that fascinated me about the prairies was the almost total absence of trees and the way one could see the faraway grain elevators, standing tall, like posts on the horizon. But as one came close enough to see the town's name in huge lettering on the elevator, it was possible then to see the town itself spread out beneath. The students talked of going to the hills for an outing, but the "hills" were mostly ravines that lay below the prairie level.

Icicles dripped and then disappeared with the last snow, and the college buzzed with a new energy. Happily sharing their plans, the students prepared to leave for the long break. Just when we thought we were the only ones who did not know where we were going, an opportunity opened up for us in Western Alberta, to assist with four country churches. By now we had enough money for a car and Gordon found a sturdy 1949 Pontiac. So when the time came to leave, we too were part of the general exodus.

With high hopes and real excitement we set off, speculating on the summer before us and talking over plans for me to enter the college in the autumn. It was my first experience of driving hundreds of miles on a straight road. The melting snow draining off the rolling prairie had collected in triangular ponds along the roadside. These "slews" were full of wild duck.

About 50 miles west of Red Deer, a town roughly halfway between Calgary and Edmonton, the four country churches were strung out along Diamond Valley. The pastor lived in a good house adjoining the largest church and generally he took services there together with another church a few miles away. We were asked to take care of the two smaller churches further out under his supervision. There was no house available at that time but accommodation, in the form of a tiny log cabin on a nearby cattle ranch, was offered to us in return for Gordon working on the ranch during the week.

I coped quite well with chopping my own wood, cooking on a wood burning stove and carrying water from a distant pump. I even coped with the rats that ate holes in my one good dress, but my pioneering spirit wavered when I realized that the toilet was across the yard next to the bullpen. Trekking across the yard in all weathers was no real problem, but I never could get used to the bull banging, huffing and blowing through the somewhat wide chinks in the log wall.

Our chief responsibility, under the Pastor's direction, was the larger of these two churches. Music was a guitar played by a ranch hand called Slim. There was no salary but the custom was for the people to give their produce if cash was short. Every now and then we were expected to take a service at an even smaller church several miles further west. Often we did not have enough petrol to go there. No matter that the congregation would load our car with an armful of rhubarb, a pail of peas or a basket of corncobs, we needed some cash. So once again I went in search of a job. I found one as a hospital laundress in the little town some twelve miles away. It only paid $90 per month but it did get us some petrol, groceries and a quantity of preserving jars to take care of the surplus donated vegetables for the winter.

Living in this rural setting fascinated us. Both lovers of the countryside, we reveled in being on the edge of the wilderness. Several times in our travels around the district we saw bears. Gordon was no stranger to dirt roads, and soon we both learned our way around. As the summer progressed, the hedgerows were a mass of wild roses.

Later that summer, the tiny log cabin manse beside the church became available and we moved in. It was a considerable improvement over the ranch situation. From our windows there was a distant but clear view of the snow capped Rocky Mountains. The congregation was of mixed European descent with enough Danish people in the area to warrant a once-a-month church service in that language conducted by a Danish circuit preacher. The people were friendly and there was time to attend church picnics, barbecues and rodeos. One night, driving home very late and being very tired, I was dozing when Gordon swerved violently and the car shuddered to a halt halfway into the roadside ditch. He said he had swerved to avoid running into a flock of sheep across the road. But there were it all was, time was short and never far from our minds was the pressure of wondering how we were going to be ready for school again.

The fact that we had not been able to save any money for school fees bore down heavier as the summer progressed. I had always wanted to study and at best, would be one year behind Gordon. Would I have to work again to enable Gordon to at least complete his studies?

Chapter 2
The King's Business

Toward the end of August, a student friend of Gordon's invited us for a long weekend to Banff in the Rocky Mountains. It was truly a great time and we enjoyed all that time would allow in the mountains. In his home church that Sunday morning, we were asked how we felt about returning to Africa once our studies were complete. We replied we were ready to go whenever the Lord called - a reply we were to be reminded of a good deal sooner than we could have dreamed.

After our return home, we grappled again with the cold facts. School started in just a few weeks, and there was again not enough money for even Gordon to go back. It was a matter of some urgency and prayer. Arriving home from church on the first Sunday in September, we found a note pinned on the door: 'Please call (a Winnipeg number) urgently'. It was a message from a pastor, at that time unknown to us, and signed by our mentor.

The nearest telephone was on a farm several miles away. All the way over there we could not help speculating. We realized Winnipeg was in a different time zone. Who there knew us? Was it a mistake? What was it about?

Once connected, the summons became clear. It was from the founder of the mission to which Gordon's friends in Africa belonged. They were faced with an emergency in Southern Rhodesia. This pastor and his wife, herself a veteran missionary who had served in China, had been praying for an answer to their problem for some time. They needed to find to a replacement for their man in Bulawayo as quickly as possible. His extensive work could not be left without a supervisor. His mother lay ill in Canada and he was long overdue for leave. About this time other missionaries from Rhodesia passed through Winnipeg and hearing of this, they suggested that we might be worth contacting. Though they had no knowledge of our situation, they did know of Gordon's deep desire to return to Africa as soon as possible.

Well of course, the pastor and his wife had never even heard of us and eagerly asked questions. Being people of great faith and godly boldness, they placed the call to Alberta. What was our position? Would we even be willing?

It was a considerable shock to be asked such a momentous question out of the blue. After a long conversation, it was agreed that we should both think about it and pray on it that night, as would the folks in Winnipeg. It was arranged that he would telephone again, to the Diamond Valley manse at noon the next day, Monday, so we could all talk together.

By that time, Gordon and I had thought through all the pro's and con's, not least of which was the financial closed door to going back to college. But we were still thinking in terms of future weeks, even months, so were considerably rocked back on our heels to learn of the proposed time scale. The call from Winnipeg came on time and we were asked how we felt about this request. Gordon replied tentatively that, in principle, we were willing and could be available. A confident response came down the line. After a night of prayer, the pastor and his wife had been put in mind of a passage of scripture from 1 Samuel 21. "The King's Business requires haste, brother," he said quoting from verse eight. "Can you leave on Thursday"

It is probably an understatement to say that our departure from Alberta was hurried. The calm acceptance and understanding of the situation by both our mentor and the two congregations where we had been working, helped enormously. We were confident in our decision, but practical matters took a little organizing. Still expecting to have some time in Winnipeg to prepare for overseas, we wisely set aside a host of speculation and concentrated on packing up. Finding that our old suitcases were damaged meant a round trip of hundred miles to Red Deer to purchase new stout cases, and that meant we did not then have enough money for the train fare to Winnipeg. The whole congregation held a farewell supper for us on the Tuesday evening, raising the money for our tickets as a gift, with a new shirt for Gordon and a blouse for me. Our heavy luggage with all our winter clothes and other things was still at the college awaiting our return. As the Canadian Pacific railroad via Red Deer to Winnipeg did not go through Saskatoon, we sent messages to the Dean of the college suggesting that our goods be distributed to any needy students. The heavy clothing we had invested in for a minimum three years in Canada was not going to be needed in Africa. We still owed a big repair bill so the garage took the car in exchange. Every problem was dealt with in a whirl of activity and the Lord's provision. On Thursday afternoon we were on the transcontinental train going east.

Not having enough money for sleepers, we alternately dozed and talked through the night reaching Winnipeg on Friday afternoon. Throughout we had supposed there would be time in Winnipeg to prepare for our new position and procure the things we needed. It was not so. Our gracious, loving hosts were on fire and plans were already made. Later that evening they explained the position in more detail. First, the matter was extremely urgent and as the work in Bulawayo was extensive, it was important that Gordon get there quickly and have a little time for their man to show him round and explain matters before handing over and leaving. Therefore an air ticket was booked through to Bulawayo, leaving early that Monday morning.

The speed at which events had moved had left the Winnipeg church without funds available to send me also. So I stayed with them with all the remainder of the luggage until such time as the passage by sea could be arranged. The mission founder had been in communication with other African missionaries on the field and colleagues in Canada, and it was agreed that despite his not having finished his studies, recognition of all he had done in Nyasaland, be given to Gordon, so that he could take up his new work with all the authority the position required.

Saturday was spent largely shopping for things Gordon needed. There was no problem about immigration because Gordon had residential status in the Federation of Rhodesia and Nyasaland. He also spoke two of the main African languages, and these things also had pointed out his suitability to fulfill this particular mission. While his time on the field and in the school had given him many skills, I was totally unprepared for the role of "missionary elect" and was nervous of public speaking. To a point, events had swept me along but on Sunday afternoon I had a real panic attack. Gordon was shut in the study being briefed. I was alone in the bedroom trying to sort our clothes out, becoming more and more distracted by thoughts of the enormity of what we were about to do. Tears ran down my face, blotching my glasses as I sat on the floor crying, trying to reach out to catch the hem of His Garment in a plea for some restoration of peace and assurance. It seemed He was in the room with me, saying, "Fear not." My anguish turned to praise, and it was as if a spring of warm water gushed up in my innermost being and washed over me, while the warm ripples ran to my fingers and toes. The room was filled with a marvelous light, very, very bright, but which did not hurt my eyes. When I got up off the floor, it was almost an hour later.

In the pre-dawn chill, Gordon flew off on the first leg of his journey, and I was left praying I would be strong enough for all that was required of me. Alone now with the old couple, I lost forever any fear of what lay ahead and eagerly waited to see how things would work out. In the days that followed I was to learn many lessons about faith that I would never forget. My hosts had said, "Now we shall see the Lord provide for you, my dear." To my knowledge, they had made no specific requests for money. Their own congregation knew about this as did the mission headquarters, although there was no spare funding from that source.

Winnipeg was the home church of the missionary in Bulawayo, and this explained their degree of involvement. Day after day, money poured in with the mail. Within a week enough was on hand for me and I happily booked my passage to Africa. Unknown to me at that time, one single gift had also been given direct to Bulawayo for a car for us. In so many practical ways I learned spiritual truths which remain vivid to this day.

Accordingly I took the train to Montreal, then ship to England. As the ship steamed down the St Lawrence Sea way towards the Atlantic Ocean, I felt the excitement of those last few days gradually settle into a calmer mood of expectation mixed with a sober resolve to do my best in the new situation. But before that could be put to the test, a new setback awaited me in England. It had been planned I should stop for a few days with my family before sailing to Beira, in Mozambique, then by train to Bulawayo. However, my letter telling my family of our move crossed with one from my Mother advising me of my father's continued decline in health. When I arrived he was in hospital due to have a major operation the next day. My mother was in some difficulties with the business, and she asked if I could stay a bit longer. Swift communications flew back and forth between Solihull, Winnipeg and Bulawayo. The result was a little time gained to be with them and to help. As soon as my father gained strength I changed my ship and train tickets and prepared to fly out, sending the heavy baggage by sea. The mission's founder and the church in Winnipeg were totally supportive and even sent me a love gift of a hundred dollars for extra pocket money.

When the day came for my departure, the connecting plane from Elmdon to London failed to arrive because of a fault, which meant I missed the flight I was booked on. It was a major anticlimax. It was on a weekend and the airways staff said they could do nothing to arrange my onward flight then. I should come back early the following day to board a flight to London, where they suggest I should report and present my ticket. It all sounded a bit daunting and uncertain.

The delay was disappointing, but there was nothing to be done about it. We trailed home, and I sent a telegram to Gordon, which later I learned did not arrive in time. My father was still convalescent and frail, and as my flight next day was very early, it was decided Dad should not turn out again. This time I made the connecting flight without any problem and in London my ticket was changed and I was airborne by that evening. In the end I arrived in Africa a day and half late. Gordon, long used to African ways, was unperturbed and he was prepared to turn up at the airport to meet the subsequent flights till I did appear.

Having been advised by Gordon that he would be there that week meeting with missionary colleagues, I flew to Ndola on the Copperbelt. It was wonderful to come from the frosty autumn fog in England into the warm velvet air of tropical Africa. To me it seemed like perpetual summer at first, but I soon learned the seasons. The richness and color of a new land and people absorbed me and I was very happy to be with Gordon again.

The rains had begun and in the town the street lamps attracted the flying ants that whirled round the lights like a snowstorm, leaving the confetti of their discarded wings to litter the pavement. Sometimes the flying insects threatened to choke the car radiator. They landed on the windshield with considerable force, leaving their squashed bodies to smear and clog up the windshield wipers. Water rushed down the culverts and the sound of the rain on the corrugated iron roof was deafening. When the rain stopped, the land steamed.

Those first few days in Ndola flew by. So many new things to taste, to see, people to meet, a new kind of church to sample. The Canadian Missionaries working on the Copperbelt of N. Rhodesia were those who had originally stayed with Gordon in Nyasaland. Now while others had taken over the work there consolidating, teaching and building, these two couples were engaged in evangelistic work with the aim of planting an indigenous church in all eight Copperbelt towns. It was my first experience of the exuberant African church, their meetings which joyfully ran practically all day with folk only pausing to eat and drink before regrouping in an ecstasy of praise and enthusiasm and who had a real hunger for the reality of God.

Then it was time to go home to Bulawayo. The journey by road south was a revelation. The new fully tarred road to the Copperbelt had only just been completed and this journey was a wonderful introduction to the Rhodesias. The long straight road stretched to the horizon. We left the heavily wooded north and ran through miombo woodland characterized by large anthills and candelabra trees. Indeed the very large anthills to be found on the Copperbelt were so high and wide; it is common practice to situate water tanks upon them to give a gravity feed to the houses. Then the more wooded north gave way to more open country as we traveled south. The sun beat down as we dropped to the Zambezi Valley, and we stopped on the bridge high over the river that was the border between North and South Rhodesia. In sweltering heat we stood looking down on the magnificent swirling waters below.

In the valley the road was an anvil under the hammer of the sun. This was hottest time of the year and no rain had fallen for eight months. The air caused the road in front of us to float in what seemed to be streams of trailing mist. I saw my first elephant, a long bull, standing motionless, under an umbrella acacia tree by what had once been a small water hole, The sound of the 'Christmas beetles", the cicadas in the trees, was like the constant sound of frying eggs.

We wound our way up the southern escarpment, came to Makuti, and stopped to stretch our legs at the café perched above the road. We sat in the shade on the patio with the panorama of Africa spread out before us. All this was not new to Gordon, but now I had fallen in love with it myself.

We went on, passing roadside vendors who patiently sat under a tree beside piles of watermelon or tomatoes. Occasionally, we would see a bullock-cart trundling along often with two or three laughing children perched on top of the load. When I saw two or three sacks of charcoal propped up with no sign of people, I asked Gordon about this. He slowed down at the next place.

"See there," he pointed to a few small huts barely visible through the trees.

"If you want to buy, you just honk your car horn and they'll come running."

So talking and learning about this new and fascinating land, we swept into Salisbury, the capital and home of our mission presbyter. As the car drew up, this jovial dear man appeared on the veranda, booming his greeting. He ushered us to meet his Norwegian born wife, saying in his usual hearty manner,

"Have you got the victory, sister?"

It was overwhelming, and I was unsure of myself in the face of much experience and bonhomie. But I learned.

The next day's journey took us through more small towns where mango trees lined the streets and life evidently revolved around the agricultural development. It was a rich rolling land of orchards and irrigated crops, cattle ranches and tobacco farms. At last in the late afternoon, we saw the blue haze of Bulawayo's jacaranda trees.

The city was second only to Salisbury, the capital. Its wide streets had been planned for huge ox drawn wagons to turn easily. Home for that first year was to be 14, Flamboyant Avenue in the suburb of Sauerstown. Our responsibilities included overseeing five farm schools which had been founded in a ninety mile radius of Bulawayo, meetings with a house group in an Asian settlement and another, mostly European, on the outskirts of the city. The meeting in the Indian household was very small, only 3-5 adults. At the first sight of our car coming through the gate, the children ran giggling to hide in the garden. Sometimes, we caught glimpses of them peeking around the doorway, but if we attempted to get their attention they scuttled off. Nevertheless, patience and prayer won the day. One of those small boys grew to be a prominent Christian leader in that land.

Sundays found us first taking classes and a service in two boarding schools, followed by a meeting in the almost finished church premises in one of the townships. There were also services to be taken at Khami, the maximum-security jail outside Bulawayo. This was a favorite with me, for although I was not allowed in, I stayed in the car under a huge shady tree near the gate and enjoyed the sheer beauty of hundreds of male African prisoners' voices raised in song which carried clearly on the warm air.

We settled into our new routine, only breaking once to accompany some colleagues on a brief visit to Durban in Natal, South Africa. It was here I learned I was to have a child, and our joy was complete.

All went well and by the time the child was due, news has come that our colleague on leave was ready to return to Bulawayo. He arrived just before the birth of our firstborn, Grace, late in October. The timing was excellent, freeing us to concentrate on the baby and prepare our next move, which was to be the Copperbelt in N. Rhodesia.

Of the two couples working for the mission the Copperbelt, one family was about to go on leave and we were asked to take their place. This time we would have to share the house with the other couple, which was at Garneton, a few miles north of Kitwe. We already knew this young couple. They had known Gordon in Nyasaland and had been my hosts when I first arrived. The work would be quite different but we looked forward to the challenge.

Before we left for the Copperbelt, we visited the schools for the last time. These five schools were small, built on farms to the south of Bulawayo. On average it took two to three hours of driving on hot, dusty, dirt roads through rather poor grazing country, an area verging on stony semi-desert. The numerous farms gates that spanned the road were opened by ragged urchins who came running through the scrub at the sound of our car. Here we found a use for the many used Christmas cards sent to us by mission groups. Short simple gospel stories or scripture verses were printed on the blank backs of the pictures. We handed these out as we passed through these endless gates and the kids loved these colorful 'thank you' tokens.

Finally, we would come to the school. The thatched one-room building, built of lime washed mud brick, stood in a clearing of swept, bare ground. An acacia tree or two gave sparse shade, together with a couple of mango trees. As our car drew up, the teacher would appear from the dim interior to greet us. Inside, light and air was provided by a simple gap about shoulder height all the way round beneath the eaves. The pupils, of various ages, sat on long rough wooden benches, girls on one side, boys on the other. We were led to the front and given the places of honor beneath the blackboard. Then we were treated to songs and chanted lessons. After a short address, the children were dismissed and we could visit and do business with the teacher.

On these farewell visits, I would return to the car at this point to attend to our daughter. It was quite disconcerting at first, getting used to breastfeeding with the car completely surrounded by curious children, jostling to press inquisitive noses through the open windows. Breast-feeding was no novelty to them, but as a white woman doing it, I was.

Grace was only three weeks old when we packed our car and headed north. I kept hovering over the carrycot on the back seat, a little anxious lest the heat of the Zambezi Valley distress the baby. But all was well, and the journey was accomplished without incident.

The aim of the two couples working out from Kitwe was to establish a church in each of the towns in the Copperbelt area. Kitwe, Ndola, Bancroft, Kalulushi, Chingola, Mufulira and Luanshya. It was their belief these churches should become self- supporting as soon as possible. Progress was slow, but this policy produced steady and enduring growth.

Early in 1960, Billy Graham visited the Rhodesias. There was great interest among the churches and missionaries. These were to be the first multiracial meetings held in the territory and there was much prayer. There had been some unrest the week before when a European lady had been dragged out of her car and murdered on the Ndola road; but now the atmosphere was much quieter in the region, and the meetings brought in a great spiritual harvest.

We attended open-air and tent meetings with Grace in her pink carrycot often stowed under the seating. Gordon and I worked with the follow-up teams, personally taking on a group of new converts from the forestry station at Mwekera, a few miles from Kitwe.

The momentous event that year was the Congo uprising. Vehicles poured over the border. Many were shot up, people fleeing for their lives. Signs were erected all over the Copperbelt pointing 'to the south'. Those able to travel on were fed and given fuel and sent on. We heard many harrowing tales. Copperbelt residents gave what aid they could, and friendships were formed then that stood the test of many years.

Often Gordon and I talked and prayed about what we should be doing and where we should live at the end of that year if we were to stay on with our colleagues in Kitwe. We needed to find a home of our own before the other couple returned from Canada. There was enough work there, and our colleagues said they would be happy to have us stay, but we were not completely convinced that it was the Lord's will for us. However, as we prayed about it, we thought we would test the Kitwe situation, so whenever we could, we looked around for alternate accommodation. But we drew a blank.

Chapter 3
A Handful of Change

The busy weeks rolled by and it was time to go to the Missions annual conference, to be held in Salisbury. Plainly we were expected with all the other couples from all three territories in the Federation of Rhodesia and Nyasaland. But as the time drew near, we were struggling financially and wondering how we could manage the cost of a six hundred mile journey.

Since arriving in Africa we had been on the same basic allowance with no extra for the baby. We had less than $150 for everything. Maintaining a car and fuel costs often depleted our cash, yet this was essential given the distances we traveled in the work. Without contacts or friends in the Canadian churches, there were no supplements or extra gifts added to our allowance though occasionally parcels were received from Ladies Mission Circles and they were always welcomed and appreciated.

We had prayed much about this and did not tell our colleagues how little we had at that time. Since this present trip was for our legitimate duties, once again we looked to God for the provision. Accordingly we went ahead with preparations for the journey. Our colleagues left a day before us to visit friends on the way, and then the day of our proposed departure dawned.

It was on a Thursday when we drove into Kitwe some eight miles from Garneton, having so little petrol in our car that we could not even drive back with any confidence. On board were our suitcases and stuff for baby Grace and some basic camping gear to see us through a night on the road if necessary. Hoping that there might be some money in the post, we could not think of anything else. We were unsure what to expect, though to expect nothing did not make sense either. It would of course, be possible to send an S.O.S. to mission headquarters for emergency financial assistance; but we had felt all along that this would not solve the underlying problem. We were in the mood to believe in God.

Once again in town we parked near the center. While not expecting anything in the post it was the only point of contact with our support. Maybe there would be something. Right then, we could not think of any other course of action. But then, doing something was better than sitting still. However, when we went to the post box there was nothing.

The baby needed feeding and changing so we drove down to a small riverside park area, prayed again and waited. Towards noon we moved back to the town center and Gordon went to try the post-box again. There was nothing. Now Gordon's shoulder's slumped, and his mind felt blank as he retraced his steps to the car.

His attention was caught by a shout. Looking up he saw a friend waving from a nearby shop front. "Gordon man, what you doing here?" A beefy hand came forward in jovial greeting. Gordon shrugged a vague answer about delays and prepared to move on.

"Not to worry, man, come in, come in."

With enormous good humor expressed in a broad Afrikaans accent, his friend, a butcher, coaxed him into the shop. Minutes later he was being ushered out. Shoving a small parcel of prime steak at Gordon and grinning all the while, he plunged a hand into his pocket and pressed some cash into Gordon's hand. "Not a lot, brother," said the jovial one, "but go with God". And with a hearty backslap, Gordon was sent on his way.

Back at the car, the gifts were received with considerable relief and thankfulness, but now other questions arose. The money, about $6., was barely enough for half the journey. What should we do? Should we attempt to go? How far would that amount take us?

A little under halfway from Kitwe to Salisbury was Lusaka. Destined to become the new capital when independence came to Northern Rhodesia, it represented the furthest we could expect to get. Having faith to go on was one thing, but no chances could be taken with a baby along. However, we had everything we needed for her. We decided to go on and so a little after midday we drove out of Kitwe heading south.

The decision to leave on that particular day was taken because we hoped to have time to enjoy a weekend of fellowship in Salisbury before the conference began, officially first thing the following Monday morning. But since no definite plans had been made, we had at least two days in hand before we would be specifically expected at conference headquarters.

That night we camped beside the road just north of Lusaka and entered the town early next day. Though we knew no one there, we had traveled through before, and so the town was familiar. Uncertain where to start and unsure what to expect, Gordon left me with the baby in the car at the central Post Office, and he went off to explore. I bought a local paper and settled down to wait.

When Gordon left the car, it was with a growing conviction that somehow Lusaka held the key, not only that day's needs but to our overall situation. After our year in Bulawayo living in someone else's house, looking after someone else's work and currently doing a similar thing in Kitwe, even sharing the house this time, he and I had been looking forward to a place of our own.

The Mission itself had not suggested anything as yet for the next year. Was the Copperbelt the right place for us? We knew Mission H.Q. would probably be interested if we wanted to come Lusaka, would it be a good idea to look for a place here? Having a couple in the central province had been discussed. To Gordon living in the town was anathema, and our work did not require us to do so. It was only a short jump from these thoughts to wondering "if that was the way ahead, how would we live and where?" He looked around and seeing an Estate Agent's office, he walked in.

He looked around for a while then the agent enquired as to what interested him. With nothing to lose, Gordon described his dream: "a nice bit of land, not too far from town and it must have good water."

The agent produced a handful of color photographs from his desk, brought in that morning, as yet un-catalogued. It was of a small cottage west of town, 27 acres, free hold at $12000. A vast sum in 1960 for a near penniless missionary!

"Nice," murmured Gordon, "but out of the question" and walked out.

Nevertheless, later he found another Estate Agent's office, and again went in. To his astonishment he found himself in the same routine. The agent fished around on his desk and produced another selection of pictures of the same place. He read off the card to which they were clipped.

"This might suit, sir, man came in first thing this morning. Nice little place about 10 miles out".

Gordon struggling with reality tried to put the agent off - "a bit too grand... not quite what I had in mind." But it was exactly what he had in mind. He turned to go, but the Agent had correctly read the expression on Gordon's face and pressed his advantage.

He offered to drive Gordon out to see the place. By now, feeling a little more buoyant, Gordon was incapable of refusing, and arrangements were made for 2 o'clock that same afternoon. "You'll not believe what's happened, Anne," Gordon's voice at the car window had my immediate attention. His news was somewhat astonishing but I had long since given up expecting the obvious.

"Look here, this is interesting," I opened up the newspaper and pointed to the middle pages and the church ads for the coming weekend.

"You're right, this might be helpful." Thoughtfully Gordon read down the column. "Hey, here's a familiar name. Now who was it that told us about this man?" His finger stabbed the page as he turned to me I peered over to look, and indeed the name was familiar.

"Look, why don't we try this number they've given, it's probably the manse," I suggested." We've nothing to lose and it might be useful." We agreed that's what we would do. We hastily found something to eat in the car and then tidied ourselves and made the baby comfortable. At two o'clock we drove round to the agent's office, and followed his car out of the town.

The road west of Lusaka wound through an area known as Bothas Rust. Originally a very large tract of land, it was settled in the early part of the century by Boer farmers who came up from South Africa in covered wagons. It had since been divided up. Lying alongside a small river, it had been bought by an Englishman who again sub-divided. This man kept the choicest piece for himself and sold off the rest. Now he wanted to sell.

The agent's car turned off the main road to the right, followed a narrow dirt road and finally entered a gateway. The driveway sloped downwards and as he approached the house, he slowed right down for us to absorb the first impact. Set against a backdrop of wild bauhinia trees covered with white blossom was a large pink-washed rondavel, with honeysuckle on the walls surrounded by lawns. The agent drew the car to a standstill on one side beside a hibiscus hedge and indicated the way round to the main entrance. Following the path round to the front of the house, we saw to our left, a flight of circular steps which rose up to a curved, shady veranda running the whole width of the house. To the right, terraced lawns fell to the river. In center view was a curved natural waterfall sparkling in the sunlight. Quite bemused now, we followed the agent up the steps, were introduced to the owners and we all went inside.

As we were shown around, it was revealed that, in addition to the original rondavel, (a typical African round thatched house with triangular rooms built round a central fireplace), there was a double-story addition built into the side of the veranda where the land fell away sharply. The only mature trees were indigenous, though there were newly planted jacaranda and nande flame trees in the garden. The land was undeveloped, except for a small citrus orchard and a kitchen garden. The river water was pure because the river rose from a spring on that same land. In addition to the land that went with the house, there was an option to buy several hundred acres, "the remaining extent" for a much lower price.

By the end of the afternoon it was apparent that the owners were anxious for a quick sale. She was pregnant and they wanted to be out of there and resettled in South Africa before the birth. But after quick consultation together, Gordon and I decided we had to tell them of our real situation. By now we were too interested to just walk away. To our surprise, the owners were not dismayed. Before leaving, Gordon and I agreed to visit again on our way north in about 8 or 9 days time.

When we finally tore ourselves away, we were both exhilarated and very tired, it was nearly sunset and darkness fell swiftly at this latitude. Our excited minds were full of visions of how such a lovely place could be used. Could it be a center for young people, a place for missionaries or other needy people to rest, or maybe it could be a Christian guesthouse? We could not tell yet. But we knew that, in principle, once this year's work on the Copperbelt was complete, we were free to form a new ministry according to God's leading. By the time Gordon and I reached town it was getting dark. We could do no more but sort ourselves out for the night.

Soberly we took stock. Because we had enjoyed refreshments at the cottage, the edge was off our hunger and we made do with the odds and ends left from the trip. We did have baby food and so after stopping at a garage to wash and brush up and fill our water containers, we drove a little way south out of town, pulled off the road and because there were so many more people about this close to the city, we slept in the car. Early the next morning we were back in town. We telephoned the pastor whose name we had recognized in the newspaper. It was Saturday.

What a welcome! The pastor's family was very generous and their children took over the baby. From the first cup of tea onwards, Gordon and I knew we had found friends. An invitation to lunch led into the afternoon. Teatime led to supper and an invitation to stay the night. Destined to become dear friends over many years, we thoroughly enjoyed their fellowship.

While Gordon and I did not reveal all the details of our situation these folks were very discerning and were not strangers to the needs of fellow Christian workers. The pastor suggested Gordon might like to call a couple of hotels in the town, offering a ride the three hundred miles to Salisbury the next day upon some payment towards fuel. This was quite a regular practice at the time. This he did with alacrity. Having told our new friends we really must leave after lunch the following day at the latest, we went thankfully to bed, looking forward to the next morning's church service where Gordon had been invited to speak briefly.

The problem was still unsolved when we sat down to lunch. The telephone rang in the hall just as we finished dessert. Our host hurried out to answer it.

"We really should be going," I said to Gordon.

"OK, but." his reluctant reply was cut off by our host's reappearance in the doorway.

"There you go, folks. That was the Grand Hotel to say they've got someone wanting a lift to Salisbury and only too happy to pay the petrol. He's waiting for you in the lobby."

"Great! Thank God for that, I'll get our cases." Gordon was on his feet, "Come on, Anne; get the baby in the car."

In the flurry of farewells and our thanks, the pastor pressed an envelope into Gordon's hand containing a small cash gift. As soon as I had the baby settled in the car, we were off.

Late that Sunday evening, we thankfully pulled into our conference host's drive with quite a story to tell. We had more cash in hand than when we had started out, we had arrived on time, owing no man, and we had seen the cottage in Lusaka.

In due course, during the Conference week, time was put aside for us to sit with the Mission Presbyter and fully explore the Lusaka question. It was the custom for the Mission Board back in Canada to actually buy the missionaries' houses. The leadership looked favorably upon our ideas that a place should be established in Lusaka, which was very strategically placed for all the territories so they were happy to endorse the plan and we were told we could go ahead.

Naturally, Gordon and I felt pleased with this outcome and we could now look forward to see the place again on our way north. We had arranged to have our next allowance paid to us in Salisbury, and so, when the Conference was over, we prepared for the return journey in a most happy mood.

Approaching the Cottage, we allowed our excitement to bubble over a bit. We made arrangements to formerly go ahead with the sale, pending our ability to come up with the required deposit. We bent our minds and prayers to this as we sped north the next day feeling we had an open door now, which God would allow no man to shut. Further proof that we were on the right track came when a Christian businessman on the Copperbelt came forward and offered to guarantee a bank loan so we could proceed with the deposit while further arrangements could be made overseas.

Unknown to us, events were taking place in Canada that would affect the Mission leadership. This, in time, would have an effect on our status in the Mission. In Winnipeg the old and revered Founder, at whose request and under whose guidance we had come to Africa, was growing frail. Following his death, a younger, dynamic man would come into leadership with different ideas. In the next few months we made the trip down to Lusaka whenever we could, to finalize arrangements and also to walk around the place praying and asking the Lord to make His will known to us.

It was on one of these brief visits, as we camped out in the empty house with very little in the way of amenities, that a missionary couple, only recently escaped from the Congo, arrived. They were making their way down to South Africa and had been told we were to be found on our property in

Lusaka. They were worn out and all they wanted was some peace and rest. They walked or sat by the river, which seemed to be all they needed. In this small event we saw by faith some indication of what God would do in this place. As soon as we could be spared from Kitwe, we moved to Lusaka permanently. We were full of confidence and hope, happily looking forward to establishing our own home at last, eager for what was to come. All we possessed made only one full car- load including the baby. We had no furniture, no bank balance, and no idea of the trials to come, only a determination and unshakeable faith for the future.

Chapter 4
Pieces of Pie

It was heaven to get up in the morning with the wind in the treetops and bird song counterpoint to the sound of the waterfall. We walked our land and worked in the kitchen garden. Slowly gathering together a few necessary pieces of second-hand furniture to make the house comfortable, we daily soaked up the peace and thought about what God's specific work would be in this place.

There was much for this *"muzungu"* (literally 'long nose', a white person) to learn. The local people were cheerful and well mannered, with many customs almost opposite to ours. When coming to my door, they would approach calling out their customary *"odi,"* then with polite patience would stand quietly waiting until one came however long it took. When entering they would just as politely sit just inside the door on the floor until invited to stand and come forward. A gift would be received with both hands and, with a delicious sense of humor, they would fall about laughing at the least pretext.

My first experience of taking a village meeting was memorable. Having to use a translator, I stood facing about fifty intent faces and completely dried up. As I sat down again, I felt the tears of total inadequacy welling up. Nevertheless, at the end of the meeting, they all came up to me, and with characteristic politeness, thanked me for coming. They gripped my hand in the African double handshake, palm to palm, the thumb gripped and then again, palm to palm, the women bobbing a curtsey as they did so.

Gordon was still doing translation and other work in support of the Copperbelt work and elsewhere. We began to speak the Gospel to folk in the district and gradually regular meetings evolved. We met our European neighbors, several of whom lived on plots along the river below us. We also visited some nearby African villages.

"Muli bwanje?" The village headman would greet us.

"Ndiri bwino," we answered, *"Kyinu?"*

"Bwerani,'" came the hospitable reply as we were ushered into a central place in the shade. Out would come a couple of carved stools, and we would be invited to sit. Gordon would talk for a while, enquiring after health, crops or cattle. Then we could get down to the business of talking about the things of God.

In Lusaka, we widened our acquaintance among other Christian workers and enjoyed interdenominational fellowship. Throughout this period Gordon and I spent a lot of time in thought and prayer with regard to the future, waiting upon a further door of opportunity.

We chose the name "Yieldingtree" for our first home. It seemed to express the ambience of our tiny valley. We made a firm decision when we read Jeremiah 17:7,8 in our devotional reading one day.

"Blessed is the man who trusts in the Lord and whose trust is the Lord. For he will be like a tree planted by water, that extends its roots by a stream and will not fear when the heat comes buts its leaves will be green, and it will not be anxious in a year of drought nor cease to yield fruit"

The existing small orchard was mostly guavas and naartjies, a southern African variety of tangerine. To this we added a small plantation of bananas. I learned about the best variety of vegetables to grow for that climate and latitude. Together, we explored the river to its source, a spring on our own land, and prayed over every acre.

Our little home was growing. We now had a dog and two hens who were a sort of housewarming gift. Between them they produced an egg a day for Grace and sometimes for pregnant me. We inherited with the property, an old two-stroke petrol engine that pumped water from the river. This drew the water up to a tank above the house. Water was heated by a 'Rhodesian boiler,' a 44-gallon oil drum on its side elevated on a brick stand which stood at the side of the house. A log fire was lit underneath and water drawn off from a pipe through the kitchen and bathroom walls. We also had a stove and a fridge, both of which ran off paraffin. Our lighting was a single line draped through the trees from our nearest neighbor. They had a diesel generator, and that was switched on from 6 pm - 10 pm.

Some way into the pregnancy, I fell down the flight of concrete steps from the kitchen to the garden. To my great relief no harm appeared to have been done to the unborn child. The hurt to my back seemed to ease after a while and once the bruises healed, I dismissed the occasional twinge. But damage had been done which was to have long-term consequences. About a month before the baby was due, it was time for the annual Conference again. This time it was to be held in Nyasaland in April, a little earlier than usual. Gordon went off leaving the baby and I in town with some American missionary friends. A week later he came back safely and three weeks afterwards a son, Stuart duly joined the family.

They day I came home from the hospital two of the local African ladies called on me. They offered me small gifts with giggled greetings, a few small eggs in a reed basket and some tomatoes on a banana leaf 'plate'. Gordon helped me work out what they were saying. It seemed that I had attained some new status. I was now '*Amayi* Stuart," the mother of a son.

It was on that visit to our friends' home that I met another American, a lady evangelist, whose somewhat flamboyant personality fascinated me as did her very strong Southern American accent. Clearly she was not in our income group. The first morning at breakfast she announced her intention of "popping downtown for a few little necessities." I imagined replacing a forgotten toothbrush and getting a newspaper. Whatever else she bought that morning, she also came back with a brand new car.

After Stuart's birth, when the lady returned from her evangelistic trip, our friends brought her out to see us one afternoon. As soon as her wiry, redheaded form came round the end of the hibiscus hedge, she threw up her hands in apparent enchantment. And once she had seen inside the house, her admiration showed no bounds.

"Oh Anne," she said in her high-pitched Southern drawl. "Oh-me-o-my, your rooms are just like pieces of pie!" Looking up, she added, in wonder "and all under a grass roof too."

With a toddler and a baby, my days were full. As yet we could afford no help, but the garden had to be tended and the grass kept down round the house because of the danger of snakes. To the east there were no farmers tilling the ground and each year 12 ft high grass grew up to our boundary, dried in the hot sun and sooner, or later inevitably burned. So fighting grass fires on our boundary became a regular feature of the dry season months.

At such a time, as soon as smoke was seen rising above the trees, all the neighbors would dispatch their gardeners and in a very short time a whole gang was on the spot to help. We soon got used to keeping a row of 44-gallon drums of water and piles of sacks handy at strategic points along the road near the boundary in that season. A wet sack was a very effective fire fighting tool, although one had to get fairly near the flames to use it which was dangerous work. We soon prepared firebreaks on our side by keeping the fence clear of grass and Gordon hired a local tractor and ploughed firebreaks at the start of each dry season.

Things deteriorated regarding our finances. I was pregnant with our third child, and we could not afford the dental treatment I badly needed. My tooth abscessed and I landed in hospital suffering from septicemia. I recovered, but was only partially reassured about the safety of the child I carried. Before I became ill, I put my one good pair of shoes in for repair, only to find, weeks later when I was well again, they had been sold to 'defray expenses,' as the cobbler did not expect me back. This relatively small incident seemed to sum up all my frustration. Since leaving Canada our allowance had not increased despite our larger family, and the need to pay the interest on the bank loan for the house deposit. Had we not been told the purchase money would come, we would have rethought the situation. But continual reassurances from our headquarters kept us pinned down. Each month promised the solution, and each month's end brought disappointment.

We carried on as best we could. We established a Sunday school at the house and invited the neighboring children and this led to yet more contact with the neighbors. After a while, we added some classes for local African women. Gordon looked after the more distant openings in the villages, although the district was not remote. Indeed it was relatively near the city; but the needs of the people were the same, whether in town or bush and this was all laying a foundation for the future work. However, no matter how many opportunities we saw, we were becoming more and more concerned about the one problem we needed to bring to a conclusion, and the one we seemed most powerless to alter. There had been no further action from Canada in the matter of our house purchase.

At Mission H.Q., the board was financially overstretched having a lot of workers out in foreign missions. Also, changes were taking place among the leadership. They were sincere in our support but at the end of the day Gordon and I were not Canadians and had no actual Canadian church backing. Having been sent out to the field to fill an emergency gap did not necessarily mean we would have the chance to return to undertake deputation work nor guarantee a future with the Mission. So the problem hung over. In 1963 we had served with the Mission for 5 years.

Matters came to a head. Grace was unwell and I was humiliated and ashamed when the doctor diagnosed poor nutrition. Clearly, we could not go on in this fashion. Something had to give.

Month after month we struggled to pay off the interest, assured that "the matter was under consideration" but after years it was worrying. While we constantly bade ourselves to have anxiety for nothing according to the Scriptures, it was puzzling not to say downright difficult.

Gordon was reluctant to get a job. He felt the mission's policy would not allow him to work. This annoyed me and we argued.

"It's nonsense to say you can't supplement our allowance when we're desperate."

"But we're not supposed to have another job, you know that," his face took on a stubborn look. I snatched a bill from the desk.

"Look at that!" I raised it in my clenched fist and shook it in his face. I was trembling and my voice rose. "A red second reminder to pay our car repair! It brings no honor to God if we can't pay a debt for something so necessary. I have no money left and I need to get groceries. What do you suggest?" I flung the offending bill back on the desk in my fear driven anger.

His eyes shifted away from mine and he mumbled, "God will supply, we should pray...." I broke across his words impatiently.

"God IS faithful, He HAS answered so many of our prayers, He HAS kept us, but don't you see? The situation has been going on for far too long. You know we are failing in the work because half the time we can't get around because we have no petrol. Car repairs, food, and stuff for the children are necessities." I found I was shaking. He ambled over to the window and stood staring at some bird on the patio. I looked at his back and strove to be calm.

"Gordon," I tried again, quietly, "don't you think that if God intended to supply everything we need, He'd be doing just that? Every month we send a report to Mission Headquarters. Doesn't that tell you something?"

"Well, what?" He half turned from the window but kept his eyes on the bird. My shoulder slumped. I was tired, despondent and frustrated. I tried again.

"Right now I don't think it matters what the Mission says, they'll probably not know. I'm not talking about anything major, may be a part-time job, anything to help us pay our bills and not constantly battle. Maybe," I added carefully, "maybe it's time for you to just be the man and work to take care of our needs, while we wait for the answer from Canada about the house." I stopped. He was silent, still looking out of the window. I waited.

"Right then. If you won't do that for us, you look after the children and I'll get a job." I turned and left the room and he let me go without another word.

Fortunately, one of our neighbors was the Branch Manager at the Dairy Produce Board in Lusaka. He not only found me a secretarial job, he offered to take me with him each day. Gordon kept the children with him and did most of the basic work at home.

Our third child was born late in 1963 to complete our family. However my health had become so undermined that after a difficult confinement, he had been born a sick baby. Although he made good progress, his early years were dogged with ear infections, dental problems and pneumonia. Gordon and I were tired, and still there was no satisfactory conclusion regarding our house purchase. We decided it was time to apply to the Mission for overseas leave, not only to get some rest and see our families, but also in the hope that it would give us a chance to talk face to face with mission H.Q. regarding our circumstances. Perhaps a visit to Canada would also give us the opportunity to bring our work to the attention of the churches and generate more support.

We had been in Africa nearly six years without a holiday. In England my father was failing, and I very much wanted him to see my children before it was too late. Since it was usual for the Mission to bring their missionaries back to Canada every five years or so for about a year, we rather expected something similar. First a period of rest - usually with one's family - then deputation travel among churches, publicizing the work on the field and thereby gaining renewed interest among our supporters.

It was a considerable surprise and disappointment when the reply came early in 1964. We were not invited back to Canada. The suggestion was made that we should have three months break in England, and money for ship's ticket from Cape Town to England would be forthcoming. There was no provision for traveling over and above our regular allowance. It was the best part of two thousand miles by road to Cape Town. Gordon went out to seek a job for travel money.

The only casual job he could find then was at the Lusaka abattoir. It was a most miserable, bloody and cold job but he gamely endured the unpleasantness. However, the disappointments were to be compounded. A friend who had kindly offered to dress-make for me so I had something nice to wear on holiday, suddenly had to cancel her offer. Her husband was on the management of the abattoir, and he autocratically bade her not to dress-make for an employee's wife. I did the best I could with the material which was already cut out, and which I had saved from a missionary parcel. My sewing machine was an ancient hand model so the results were not very good. Indeed I did not have time to finish them.

Baby was six months old when we set off. All our personal stuff was locked into one room and the cottage let to cover the bank payments during our absence. Although latterly we had been pressed by the bank to improve on our arrangements, we had put them off pending our return. Perhaps when we rested in England, we could once again address the problem. Perhaps we could write again and appeal clearly for a definite assurance regarding the house purchase. Certainly we badly needed to have the position reassessed never for a moment thinking it could get worse.

Our departure was plagued with delays. Allowing so many days to drive to Cape Town to catch the ship to England, we moved out of the house to allow our tenants to move in and spent two nights at a friend's farm. To travel so far by road with three young children took some planning. I overhauled the children's clothes because I knew there would be little spare cash for shopping in England - though some money had to be held in hand for warm clothes. On the last morning while trying to finish the packing, I was distracted by the need to go look for Grace and Stuart when I realized it had gone very quiet. I tracked them down on the far side of a nearby banana plantation happily squatting beside a small stream. They were floating Grace's new little white shoes as boats. But the day was not over yet.

Not long after lunch, while Gordon was in town preparing the car, I was busy settling baby down for a nap when I head shrieks coming from outside. Rushing to the window I saw Grace and Stuart cowering against the wall. The farm family had kept a monkey chained to a pole in the yard. Now it was loose. Stuart who was not yet three years old had been bitten in the leg and was screaming. Before I could get outside, the monkey jumped through the open window into the cot and snatched the baby's bottle from his mouth.

Now I was screaming, and, without thinking, I grabbed a hand towel and flapped wildly at the monkey. Chattering furiously, the money leaped onto the dressing table sending everything on it flying. The uproar brought the indoor staff on the run, and, after the expenditure of more sweat and noise, the animal was finally ousted. Clutching the screaming baby I rushed to attend to Stuart who had been bundled into the hall by his sister. Both were still convulsively sobbing. Gradually everything calmed down. After a soak in antiseptic, the wound looked clean enough, and I had no particular misgivings. In any case, I could not do any more right then. Gordon had not yet returned with our car and the other farm vehicles were away. The farm was at least twenty miles away from a doctor. Indeed the wound itself never did fester and healed over in a few days. But that night, Stuart woke up with what looked like heat bumps all over his body.

It was a very doleful toddler that was packed into the car next morning. Covered from head to food in Calamine, he experienced a most miserable journey. For as soon as the effects of the Calamine wore off, more bumps seemed to appear. We stopped in the little town of Gwelo and sought a doctor, but he didn't have any suggestion to offer. "Just keep using the Calamine," he said. Again in Bulawayo, another doctor still had no solution. The wound was healing cleanly, but some of the unexplained bumps were beginning to blister. In vain, I repeated to the doctor that the only unusual thing to have happened was the monkey bite. I stocked up on calamine.

It was a long journey, and we had to make up the time. After Bulawayo, there was no time to stay the night, if we were to catch the ship. Our Chevrolet was ideal. We had taken out the back seats and on the platform behind the bench front seat; we piled blankets, quilts and pillows, added a few storybooks and toys and piled the children in. It was a two- door car with an extended back to take the luggage together with car tools, an extra tire and a large water container.

We picnicked as we drove, and just before sundown each day, we pulled off the road in a safe place and let the children run about while we shook out all the blankets and quilts and remade their bed in the back. We fed the children, and, filling the bowl we carried from our large water container - which was tepid from being in the sun, I sponged the children completely down, covered Stuart with calamine and put them all back in the car in their night-clothes. Then we were off again.

One by one the children fell asleep. Later we pulled into a motel, ate a hot meal, washed, and brushed up. Our Thermoses were filled with boiled water for the baby's bottle. We topped up the car with petrol, and replenished the big water container. We drove away in well under an hour and took turns driving through the night.

The rains had ended and we drove south through the increasingly dry terrain. We crossed the Limpopo River into South Africa, pulled into Messina for lunch and pressed on. The road was lined with white and mauve cosmos, the country rolling away to distant blue hills. Then Pretoria fell behind us, and we drove down the map on the verge of the great Karoo desert, through another night and on until we saw the mountains of the Cape.

Finally, on the last lap, we pulled into Worcester not long after dawn. There we had a contact who offered to keep our car until we returned. We still had about 70 miles to go, but as he drove us through the vineyards, we gave thanks for a safe journey. We had made it to the ship with only a couple of hours to spare.

Our poor toddler was under the ship's doctor's care the whole way to England. Now he was a mass of blisters, but he was amazingly good. I kept him in thin soft cotton clothes and did everything possible to keep him as comfortable as I could. But nothing really helped.

As soon as the ship docked, we were met by my brother and driven to Solihull where I took Stuart to my mother's doctor's surgery by 5:30 pm that same day. But still we battled on for another three weeks. In despair, we told some missionary friends who were on leave from the Congo. At their suggestion, the advice of an herbalist was sought. To our great relief but total amazement a remedy costing a dollar was advised and tried. The blisters dried up and healed in a week. It transpired a year or so later, on sharing this experience with a veterinary friend with some knowledge of transporting zoo animals, that the dangerous secretions in the saliva of an excited monkey could have been lethal.

Chapter 5
A Box of Matches

It was not until just before Stuart's third birthday in May that the final answer came from Canada. Since we were English, would we not consider remaining in England? They advised us that financial support would cease in three months as the Mission Board considered they were overextended both in finance and workers on the field. They hoped the three months notice would be acceptable. However, when the initial shock receded, and we thought back over the very long period of procrastination regarding our house purchase, we found we were not really surprised. Perhaps our unique situation within the Mission had all along been part of God's Plan for us. But the circumstances we found ourselves in left us in a real dilemma. We had wanted and been willing to work in Africa, answering the Mission's call in good faith. Now with a family to support, what should we do? Believing ourselves in God's will, we had begun a work in Lusaka, and we had to either extract ourselves from our responsibilities there at long distance, or go back completely on our own and see it through.

Not least of these problems was Gordon's real reluctance to give up everything we had started in Africa and to have to get a job and housing in England. There was no money, in any case, for Gordon to go to Lusaka and back to settle our affairs while I hung on in England with the children. It was heartbreaking in the light of our conviction that Lusaka was where we were meant to be. We decided to go back.

Setting sail in the S.S. Capetown Castle, we reached Cape Town towards the end of July. It had been a good trip despite the uncertainties of what lay ahead. Our tickets had covered all our food, so it was possible to enjoy the trip with almost no additional costs.

As we had done on the outward trip, we booked ourselves in for the second sitting for dinner at night, so we could settle the children in the cabin after their early evening meal under the eye of our steward. But on the first night out from Southampton, our wily eight- month old second son would not settle. In desperation I bundled him up and took him in with us to dinner where he ate his way through two bowls of ice cream while smiling and bouncing on my lap to the delight of our companions at the table. For the next eleven nights at sea, as the other two sleepily keeled over, promptly he would be sitting up bright as a button, confidently waiting for us to take him down for more ice cream and entertainment.

Our friends were on the dock to meet us in Cape Town and we went with them to Worcester for the night. Now we had only $30 remaining in cash and faced a journey of almost two thousand miles. There was one allowance, the final one, to look forward to on arrival. By this time some fatalism had crept into our thinking. Either we had interpreted our situation correctly in the light of our beliefs, prayers and what we knew of God, or we were completely wrong and would come badly unstuck. We would keep going and test the outcome. We knew that Gordon could find employment in N. Rhodesia, possibly more easily than in England anyway, if we could get back there.

We packed the car and headed north. Our resolution was about to be tested indeed. It was now mid-winter in the Cape and the wind coming off the mountains had a bitter edge. Our sturdy car had been second-hand when Gordon bought it on arrival in Bulawayo. It had been in excellent condition but our extensive mileage on consistently rough roads was taking its toll. The car was in its ninth year and beginning to show the odd frailty.

The first night we slept in the car and the next on the garage floor of a very small town manse. The pastor and his wife were generous providers of a good breakfast, so our little party in the dusty Chevrolet went on in good heart.

The car finally broke down in one small South African town. We had no money for repairs so it was imperative that we find a garage willing to trust us and wait for payment. This was not so extraordinary as it sounds. In the 1960's it was still possible to do such a thing because there was a great deal of traffic moving up and down between South Africa and the territories in the far north. We were still a little more than a thousand miles from home. To our great relief we found such a garage and, when later in the afternoon the car was ready again, we discovered in conversation with the proprietor that he was a Christian. Not only did we all enjoy a few minutes fellowship but he then waived the bill and sent us off with his blessing. We thanked him and thankfully praising God we pressed on.

It was extremely cold as we climbed to the high veldt. That night in Johannesburg was memorable for a late-night fall of snow. Again we had found a church and gratefully accepted a night's shelter in the manse, but we had to remain fully clothed and huddled up together to keep warm. There was one more stop before crossing the Limpopo River at an address given to us by our hosts in Johannesburg. We had sweet fellowship and a very good night's rest. They pressed a cash gift into our hands to take us the rest of the way, but unknown to us; our youngest brought something else away with him. As we drove away we were unaware that we carried measles with us.

Another night, in Bulawayo with our colleague and again a night in Salisbury with our Presbyter and once again we came home.

It was no easy task we had set ourselves. The first priority was to ensure we had money to live on while we planned the future. Gordon went job hunting. His experience was in farming yet he did not want to leave our property in West Lusaka and move away, nor did he wish to live away from the family, so he looked for something allied. He found a vacancy in the milk bottling plant of the Dairy Produce Board on the main street in Lusaka, Cairo Road. Within the month he was installed as assistant manager and since dairy was his forte, he quickly assimilated other skills and the first hurdle was over. I also considered taking a job but when the three children went down with measles, one after the other, I found myself grounded.

With the pressure on to keep up our house payments, we had to borrow to pay for groceries to tide us over until we received the first salary check. The job took an enormous load off our minds but took a lot of adjustment. Gordon began his day shortly after 4.00 am to start at the factory by 5 am. It was a considerable blessing when he had swift promotion to Factory Manager, although he still began the day at the same time. But before that, the hand of fate fell heavily again.

During this period, N. Rhodesia had been gearing up for the celebrations that would herald the new nation of Zambia. There was a great air of expectancy in the country. Rehearsals for the ceremony at the city sports stadium were in full swing.

Ten days beforehand found us preparing to receive friends from England. They were coming to work on a large poultry franchise to the east of Lusaka. On arrival they were given a car but their accommodation was not quite ready, so it was arranged they came to us in the meantime. To make room for this family of six, we cleared the bedrooms in the main house for them while we moved with our children into the guestroom downstairs which had its own bathroom. Their oldest child was aged seven and the youngest, ours, barely one. They all had a wonderful time together, but a devastating blow was about to throw us all into turmoil.

On Monday morning October 19th, after dropping Gordon off at the milk factory, Tom went to his new job. A little later I took our car into a garage in the city for servicing and then went shopping. Back at the house, Jenny was keeping an eye on all seven children. Near the little church at the edge of our property a small African boy was playing with a box of matches and laughing with excitement as the grass verge caught fire. His amusement turned to terror as the church caught fire. After several months of completely dry weather everything was combustible. With a roar the little church was consumed and the wind caught up the burning thatch, blew it across the ploughed firebreaks and it fell directly on to the thatched roof of our house.

When Jenny realized what was happening, her first thought was for the children. It took a while to account for them all, but she pushed them out of the house and told them to run down to the river. By the time she scooped up the seventh child, our precious baby, the ceilings and curtains in that room were alight. By that time our only worker had come running and it was not long before the neighbors' workmen arrived and joined in. But little could be done. There were only one or two things saved from the kitchen extension, which had a corrugated iron roof.

When the smoke rose above the trees, it was spotted by our nearest neighbor. She first dispatched her gardeners, then drove over and took Jenny and the children into her house. None of them were injured or burned, but all were in a considerable state of shock. Then they telephoned Gordon at the milk factory and he in turn contacted Tom at the poultry farm. The Branch Manager of the Dairy Produce Board threw his car keys at Gordon and just said, "go". The two men arrived almost together to a scene of ruin, but there was little they could do. The house was a smoking heap of debris. The whole scene looked so strange as roundabout the house the trees had contained the fire and it had not spread, but surrounded by the still verdant garden, lay this stinking gray mass of all the possessions of our two families.

Gordon went back to town looking for me. At the garage he found the car not yet ready but saw my shopping where I had left it at the office and guessed I had gone off to find a cup of tea while I waited. At our usual café, I looked up and saw him approach. I felt a brief moment of foreboding at his expression and could only think he had lost his job. Time seemed to stand still as he sat down and was obviously searching for the right words to tell me something dire. My expression must have conveyed my anxiety for he quickly told me the children were okay, and then went on to explain what had happened. It took some minutes for the news to sink in, but I latched on to the fact that the children were unharmed which was my chief concern. We collected our car, returned the borrowed one to the factory and very soberly drove back to what had been home.

The workmen had done all they could. Some had brought water up from the river in an effort to save the kitchen extension but it was badly damaged. Everyone was subdued. Small spirals of smoke rose here and there above the deep piled ash. The breeze had blown bits of debris and ash across the garden and the soot covered men stood around in sweaty exhaustion. Feeling shocked and spent we went over to our neighbor to join Jenny and the children. There were tears and hugs all round and then with welcome cool drinks, the grown-ups sat down to think. It was barely lunchtime.

After making telephone calls to their places of employment, the men returned to the ruins to keep an eye on things, Jenny stayed with the children with our good neighbor and I went back to town to get some emergency supplies. We needed eleven of everything; toothbrushes, towels, soap, First Aid. A new bucket for drinking water, basins, food and a few basic clothes for the children, blankets and diapers. The list was endless, but fortunately, we already dealt with a good general store and I was allowed thirty days credit. Laden and tired out, I drove back in the late afternoon to find the place a hive of activity.

Neighbors had sent blankets, paraffin lamps, pots, dishes and food. Two cars on the drive were unloading a six-bed tent from Gordon's boss and they erected it to one side of the lawn. Clean straw was being laid on the floor of the open sided small barn, a short distance from the house. Before dark, order of a sort prevailed. Our mood was overwhelmingly thankful that all the children were safe.

Nightfall, which comes suddenly in the tropics, found us all nevertheless, physically and emotionally exhausted. We were filthy dirty from the ash, but somehow we got cleaned up and after something to eat, thankfully bedded down. Tom and his family had the tent and we wrapped up our children between us on the straw in the small barn.

The next day was baby's first birthday. Throughout the day people called in with gifts and messages. Jenny and I organized temporary kitchen facilities in the tool shed next to the barn, did some necessary laundry at the river and generally tried to make a better job of our makeshift quarters. A pile of donated clothing needed sorting, a couple of donated mattresses improved our bedding arrangements in the barn. A friend brought a casserole dinner ready cooked, someone else even brought a cake. Friends from one of the city churches came out bringing a gift of two Bibles for us.

A farmer friend sent a tractor over with a load of useful odds and ends, tools and equipment. Tom found that although damaged on the outside, the paraffin refrigerator from the kitchen would still work. This was brilliant and it was quickly cleaned and installed in the old tool shed and, because our fire had knocked out the party telephone line we shared in the district, it had been reported before we even thought about it. So to our delight the Telephone Company arrived and installed a new telephone, again in the tool shed.

What a mood of optimism that generated! We kept telling each other how thankful we were that the children had been spared as we all pitched in with a will to make ourselves as comfortable as possible. We bought an old paraffin stove and fixed that up, but our bathroom was still the river or a bucket of water.

That night, thunder rumbled in the north and the night sky was lit from time to time with distant lightening. The rains were coming.

The men returned to their jobs. Jenny and I worked hard each day sorting and altering some of the donated clothes. In the temporary shed/kitchen we took turns preparing food One day Jenny made cakes for the children's tea, a feat that I regarded with unqualified admiration in those circumstances.

The only piece of furniture to survive the fire was a heavy square low table. We had taken it into the garden for tea the day before the fire. At dusk the men had picked up the chairs while we mothers followed along with the children, all of us content to leave the table for the time being knowing there would be no rain that night, nor likelihood of any dew this late in the dry season. So after the fire, we found it there, standing beneath the orange tree, its polished surface unmarred except for a little wind-blown ash.

Very conscious of the approaching rains, we tried to improve our living space and tried hard to think of ways to secure what we had. Jenny knew it would not be long before her family could move to their house at the poultry farm, whereas I had no such hope. The barn was particularly vulnerable to the weather as it had three open sides. Though we called it a barn it was merely a rough thatched roof extension of the tool shed, held up by four brick pillars. We made barriers with some of the donated corrugated iron roofing sheets, boxes and plastic sheeting, keeping the space next to the one brick wall shared with the tool shed, for our bedding area.

More gifts arrived, among them was a very old but serviceable treadle sewing machine, which was enormously helpful. On the other side of town the workmen hastened to complete the work on Tom's house on the poultry farm. Within a few days, the family moved there and we moved into the tent. There was still a lot of stuff piled in the barn as our only storeroom. Zambia's Independence Day came and went almost unnoticed. Then after eight months of dry weather, the rains broke.

Storms had been building up, day after day in towering clouds, heralded by deafening thunder. Forked lightening brilliantly lit up the darkening skies. One could hear the first rain coming, and then smell the first moisture on the arid breeze. The first swollen drops plopped onto the hot hard earth, and swift behind them came the first refreshing wave of moist air, then the gray blinding downpour. The rain beat everything down in its path, pouring off every surface, rushing down every slope and filling every crevice. Debris swirled in the flooded lane beside the barn and steely rods of water poked through every weak spot in the barn's old thatch.

It was difficult to keep our things dry in those first storms. Constantly on the alert for new leaks, we frequently had to move our stores about in the battle to keep everything dry. Often during a long downpour, the temperature would drop considerably and the children had to be kept warm. It was necessary to dig a trench around the base of the tent to channel off the water. The children could not play out in the drenched grass and had to be carried over it one at a time whenever a move was necessary. Nevertheless, the rain rarely lasted all day and once it ceased, the sun shone and the moisture hungry land quickly absorbed the residue. For a brief moment, droplets sparkled on every hanging branch and leaf while the eager earth drank, then all was dry and hot again.

Chapter 6
Running the Race

Time flew by as we engaged in the daily battle to keep the children healthy and secure. Although Gordon was now promoted to Factory Manager at the milk bottling plant, we needed more money. I found a job in a small engineering office in the city and day nursery places for the children. We bought another car for me, as our working hours were not compatible.

One morning I went to baby's cot to find him as limp as a rag. He could neither sit up nor suck when I tried to give him a drink. Terrified, I ran with him to the car and raced into town for the doctor who arranged his admittance into hospital immediately. The Sister in charge of the children's ward was a local Pastor's wife whom I knew slightly. She was very kind and reassuring.

When I eagerly hastened to collect my baby about a week later, he did not notice my entry at first. He was standing up at the cot rails with his back to me jabbering away at a little girl in the next cot. I tiptoed up behind him and softly spoke his name. His head whipped round and his arms were up in an instant to be held in my arms.

I was told his collapse was probably due to the delayed shock following the fire producing a sudden, severe anemia. The Doctor gave me no other explanation. Our daughter suffered nightmares for a period in the months following the fire, with rashes and occasional nervousness. But soon these tokens of that stressful time faded away and all three children were remarkably well considering our situation.

As the rains progressed, everything became sodden. Often I had to carry the children from the tent over the wet grass straight into the car so they started off dry and clean. Dry days, especially at the weekend were such a relief. The children raced around getting their kinks out while I aired blankets, turned out the tent and washed our clothes. Gordon was able to get to outside jobs although he often had to work at the weekend. He constructed a chicken house and a rabbit pen and worked in the garden.

It was a time of relentless effort that stretched into years. Grace started school in January 1965. I worked a similar schedule for four years as, in their turn, the boys followed her. But by then we did have the beginnings of a house around us although there was a long way still to go. Slow and hard as it was at the time, and because we paid cash for all our building material as we went along, we ultimately achieved a home whose value far exceeded what it cost.

The stability and peace in the country was a great blessing throughout this period. True there had been a few isolated disturbances prior to Independence, but Zambia's peace loving culture prevailed. Regular police patrols from the police post at West Lusaka, usually policemen in pairs cycled through the area. They called at each property with time to stop and talk and, if necessary, allow us to voice any concerns, which were duly reported.

Zambia's independence was soon evident in the changing of street and place names, especially those with a particular British flavor. For instance, Bancroft became Chililiabombwe (place of frogs), and Livingstone Road in Lusaka became Cha Cha Cha Road, though Livingstone town kept its name.

Our water was raised from the river by a small 2-stroke petrol pump that was in place at the time we took over the property. This pump was now aging and had several times been damaged by flash floods. It was becoming increasingly difficult to keep it running smoothly. During the rains the water often carried a lot of sand so it was not surprising that our bed sheets took on a sandy hue, despite my efforts to sun bleach them. Care had to be taken to iron everything, most of all the children's things because of the putsies. Putsi flies lay their eggs on damp cloth. If not killed off by a hot iron, the eggs, too small to be visible to the naked eye, will hatch on one's skin and the resulting grubs will burrow under the skin to cause an abscess.

Our day started with the alarm clock going off at 4.00 am and Gordon went off to work. I would get up, get the charcoal iron going and prepare one set of clothes for each of us, polish the children's shoes and pack three snack packs. Then I would go outside to put whatever spare eggs, tomatoes etc. I had into my car to sell around my office. Back to the house, to wash and dress the children, give them breakfast and prepare myself for the day's work. By 7.00am we were on our way to town where I dropped Grace off at school, then drove the boys to their day nursery, then back to my office.

As time went on my hands were often shaking with fatigue by the lunchtime. At Grace's age, school finished at 1.00pm and the day nursery collected her and kept her till I finished work. This arrangement cost nearly a third of my wages, but it included first Grace, then the boys as they went to school. They were given lunch and kept safe until I arrived. It was extremely good value and gave me absolute peace of mind, especially if at any time they were ill. The supervisor would phone me at my office, perhaps to agree to consult a doctor or to warn me to obtain medicine before leaving town that evening.

Each lunchtime after a quick snack, I went out to buy supplies, food for us and our few animals, cement and a whole host of building material. Now and then I went to the timber yard where a huge pile of discarded wood off-cuts lay in a corner of the yard. There I was allowed to rummage for useful pieces and grew quite good at spotting the potential in scrap wood of various sorts. Sometimes I pulled out of there with a considerable load topped off with a few sacks of sawdust for our chicken house floor. Our Chevrolet, with its extended back taking up to a half-ton load, became our workhorse. In time this sturdy vehicle's engine drove three and one half times round the clock before the bodywork succumbed to the ravages of time, and then it was used to run a generator.

Back at the office, I worked until 4.30pm, collected the children and drove home. The children raced round when it was dry while I looked around to see if Gordon was home yet, talked to our worker as he unloaded the car and generally made the best of that last hour of daylight. Then it was suppertime, bed and round again.

Often Gordon did not get home with daylight to spare. He usually worked part of the weekend and often on public holidays. There were often delays in the arrival of milk tankers from the depot at Mazabuka, a town 80 or so miles to the south, breakdowns of tankers and machinery of all sorts, plus power cuts in the rainy season. At least that was not a bother to me because we used gas-lamps and candles and cooked on a bottled gas stove.

Afterwards, I was to look back and realize that it was during this time that Gordon's periodic anger began to show. Perhaps the pressure had affected him in a way I knew nothing of, but sometimes he would disappear without explanation or lash out in anger without an apparent reason. As the children grew, his discipline of them was at times so physically heavy that it greatly distressed me. My efforts to remonstrate had no effect. Indeed on one memorable occasion he turned on me and actually grabbed me by the throat. This frightened me and although the episode slipped behind us in forgiveness and later calm, nevertheless it became a shadow that lurked to gnaw at my peace of mind whenever he showed anger again.

Life became a series of compromises in practical matters, making do. The children's welfare came first. As the walls went up, water was stored in buckets for cooking and drinking, a tin bath stood on bare concrete beside a four-gallon bucket for bathing, supplemented by kettles heated on the stove. Clothes were washed in the river to save hauling that water up to the house. We moved our beds, stove and stores around the builder. The long dry season was a great boon. Also Zambia's winter was only a couple of months of cold nights and the majority of days remained sunny; the children could play out.

The children were amazingly resilient. So long as I did not forget the Jolly Juice, that brilliant alternative to blackcurrant cordial and a drink that was fast becoming part of the Zambian scene, fed and cuddled them regularly, and also prayed over them unceasingly, they flourished. Even our little one's recurrent illness responded well to medication and he bounced back every time.

Towards the end of the third year after the fire, we employed a nearly full-time Zambian builder. Our poultry and garden produce was increasing, so I went to working mornings only. This meant I still did not get back from town until early afternoon but I could spend the remaining time on what, by then, resembled an English smallholding. We had a much bigger garden, more chicks and I had developed the rabbits to dress and pack for a city supermarket. I brought periodic batches of new-hatched Aylesbury ducklings up on the train from S. Rhodesia and produced table ducks. We bought a milk cow and then some week-old calves at a farm sale, raised them and sold them on at a profit.

"*Njoka! Njoka! !* Our worker shouted as he ran past the house. I could hear a bird chattering the alarm in the tree outside the kitchen window. No doubt there was snake in the tree threatening her nest. The cry of "snake" promised more excitement than hoeing and weeding so in a flash the other two gardeners came running. Excitedly they danced around the tree throwing stones in typical fashion. Their missiles were not seriously life threatening but the snake gave up anyway and soon slithered off while the disconsolate gardeners trailed back to the weeds.

The road from the farm out to the main road is a sandy track, graded once a year if we are lucky. The theory was that the cost of the grade should be shared by all who lived on the road but it did not always work out. In the year that we first came, there had been a sighting of a leopard, but after that no game save an occasional duiker, but as the population grew in the district, there was nothing except cane rats, mongoose and otters that frisked on the river. There were plenty of ants. In our early days, the red ants would sometimes swarm and devour our rabbits, leaving only bones behind them. These ants are lethal to anything penned, which cannot flee as the ants came marching in. We learned to spray circles of ant killer round each livestock pen. It is a fairly common sight to see columns of ants marching across the road. They are particularly nasty in the garden where the children can stumble on them and so stand screaming to be rescued from their swarming painful bites.

But there are gentle things too. Often as we drive home after dark, there is Venus the brightest and first evening star, sitting low on the western sky.

Our car headlights reflect the big saucer eyes of bush babies in the trees and the lawns sparkle with fireflies. The rainy season brings to us a constant chorus of bullfrogs down in the river. Tiny jewel-like tree frogs are readily seen amid the foliage and there is an abundance of colorful insects, butterflies and moths. The children loved the large brown millipedes that obligingly curled into balls when touched. A Spotted Eagle Owl regularly nested and raised her young in a hollow of an old tree beside the house.

Much to the delight of the children, a troupe of vervet monkeys who frequent the riverbank, periodically gambol through the orchard and across the lawns, even venturing right up to the trees which grew next to the house. The resulting commotion of shrieking, chattering monkeys and barking dogs never fails to draw the children to the windows to watch the fun.

For four years after the fire, we did not take a vacation. Our respective employers allowed us to take our holiday allowance in cash instead while we worked on. The fire insurance money had been paid directly off our mortgage and now, toward the end of this period we were able to pay off the remaining portion of our mortgage. The free hold title deeds were ours. In 1968 we planned our first real break and took the children to South Africa for the Easter school holidays. Gordon reveled in a weekend to spend at the Rand Easter Show, the biggest, most prestigious agricultural show in sub-Sahara Africa. We camped and wandered down to Natal and the sea, and even managed a couple of nights at the Four Seasons Hotel in Durban before visiting the Kruger National Game Park. Then we made our way back through eastern S. Rhodesia and so home again.

It was a grand time. Three weeks of refreshment and leisure, but it served only to give us our second wind. Within a few weeks, I was conscious again of an underlying exhaustion and Gordon fell ill with a series of throat infections, and this forced him to leave the dairy.

However, before he did this, I had ceased to work in town because I both wanted to be home for the children more and to increase the productivity of our little farm enterprise. Although we now had a small financial return in addition to quite a lot of our food, the loss of his salary seriously slowed us down. Still trying to complete the basic building, we had not even reached the point of installing indoor plumbing and electricity, to say nothing of ceilings, decorating or any furnishing beyond the most basic necessities. We were a very long way indeed from curtains and cushions.

For the fifth time since the fire, pneumonia hit our youngest. I bundled him into the "poorly" quilt and drove to the doctor in town. The quilt, one of several sent to us from a church sewing circle in Canada after the fire, was made in a pattern of big plain squares. Each square had been embroidered with simple short scriptures such as "He cares for you" and the like. I had started the tradition of putting this quilt on the bed when one of the children was sick, with the writing facing them so we could make a game of reading the words.

At home I put him to bed and he sat flushed, with his fair straight hair more on end than ever. Six years old Stuart climbed on to the bed, and in an attempt to cheer his brother up said, "Don't worry. If you die I expect you'll have the most famous cowlick in heaven."

"Its okay," replied the woeful four-year old, "I'll be able to help God make the butterflies."

Just before Christmas that year, the telephone rang just as I was decorating an evergreen bough as a substitute Christmas tree. It was the news that my Father had died. Suddenly overwhelmed with profound sadness and a desolate weariness, it seemed England was indeed very far away.

It was during this time of rather low spirits that we were given two gifts, both of such intrinsic value as to be ever afterwards remembered for their loving thoughtfulness. As encouragement they were priceless. One was a pair of new armchairs sent by a friend and the other was the gift of time, all the more delightful because it was unsolicited.

One Saturday afternoon when we were too hot and tired to do more, we were slumped in our chairs amid all the rubble and mess of what was to become our sitting room. Stacked against the walls were some doors, including the exterior doors, all waiting to be hung. The toolbox lay open but it was too big a job to tackle single-handed. We stirred at the sound of a car outside and went to the doorway.

"Hello the house," a friend from church called out. "Hi Anne, how are you doing?" He slammed the car door shut and pocketed the keys. "We have come to see if we can give you folks a hand. This is George," he waved a hand towards a tall man heaving a toolbox from the back of the car, "and you know Peter? " The third man grinned and extended a brown hand to Gordon.

"Oh, this is wonderful," I exclaimed trying to prevent the children from climbing up their legs. George hefted the toolbox over the step and looked around, hand on hip.

"This is going to be great. Right, let's get to it."

"Anne, keep the kids out of the way," Gordon said, his face lit up with renewed energy. I was only too happy to comply and only returned briefly to ply them with mugs of tea from time to time. By nightfall, the doors were all hung and we had reached another milestone.

Window frames for the new house were a big item. Unable to touch our burnt out building because of the long wait for insurance settlement, we were glad of a gift of several second-hand frames including a wide, curved homemade frame we used to make a bay in the new sitting room. We also obtained a cheap job lot of frames from another fire-damaged property. Cost governed every decision we made. For our bathroom, we used a tall, narrow frame that did seem suitable to go anywhere else, thinking it did not matter. Its sill was only about two feet off the floor so we could easily step over it.

Because most of the window frames were second-hand, many also fire damaged and out of alignment, it proved difficult to fit the glass cut in standard sizes. We made several trips back to town for individual trimming of almost every pane before fitting was complete. Now the house though still under thatch, had reached near completion, having three bedrooms, lounge, dining room, a large kitchen, bathroom and store. Parts of the old burned out house were subsequently renovated to provide two more rooms and another bathroom.

When the new roof went on, some years later, we purposefully extended the eaves to provide shelter all round the house so windows could stay open even in rain. The low bathroom window became very useful and even amusing. In time the family regarded it with real affection. Many were the times when we drew the car right up to our bathroom to transfer luggage, shopping, children and sleeping babies dry into the house. Once carrying a sleeping baby we crept out this way in the middle of the night to avoid the threat of armed robbers. A visitor got a big fright when she sat, happy in the bath, unaware that the window was open behind the long curtain. One of our Friesian cows stuck her huge head in the window and bawled right in her face. When we just fell about laughing instead of coming to her rescue, our shrieking guest was not at all pleased.

Late in 1968, through a friend working in a big mission school to the south, Gordon heard that they needed a teacher for their Agricultural Science program to tide them over while they applied for one to come from overseas. This subject was introduced into the schools in Zambia with the idea of giving students the rudiments of self-sufficiency. One weekend we made a trip out to the school.

The whole station was quite large with many auxiliary artisans working alongside the mission staff, both expatriate and Zambian. It was nearly a hundred miles south of our home and comprised a junior and senior school, farm and gardens. During this visit Gordon agreed to take on the job. Because of the distance from us, the timetable was amended so all his classes were scheduled at the beginning of the week, and he could leave home on Sunday evening and return by Tuesday night.

Whether it was because he was not a trained teacher that they could not offer a proper salary or what, but I only found out later he had agreed to work for petrol costs only. Despite my pointing out the obvious in this highly unsatisfactory arrangement, he was determined. Gradually his leaving time slipped forward to early Sunday morning, then he began to return on Wednesdays, often late in the day. It was not only the loss of money that was hard, but his support in practical matters was gone four days out of seven.

I keenly felt his absence, as did the children. There were lots of times when I needed him. One day the children and I came home from town and I stopped the car outside the house. I went round to unload the shopping from the back of the car. The children, as usual, had already climbed out and run ahead round to the garden. As Grace started screaming I dropped the groceries and flew round the end of the house. There in front of three petrified children was a snake in the middle of the path. For one heart stopping moment I thought it already struck.

As my mind scrabbled to assess the danger, our dog rushed forward to greet the children, putting herself between them and the snake. Somehow I snatched the children back and retreated. The dog howled and ran off. The snake disappeared. Later, when the children were having their tea, I went to look for our dog. I found her in the bushes at the edge of the garden. She was dead.

That night in our prayers we thanked God for our faithful pet. We remembered all her funny, loving ways, her excitement when she chased the monkeys, how she romped when she startled a monitor lizard down by the river one day, and how she used to bark at the gardener when he wore his bright check socks. That day, she had been God's instrument of protection, coming in time to take that lethal strike.

On another occasion after sitting up late one night, I crept into the sleeping children to check on them. To my dismay, I saw a snake between their beds, rising up the edge of Stuart's blanket. In my panic I saw nothing handy to use as a weapon. I was too frightened to leave the room to look for one. In desperation I prayed against it in Jesus' name, and then watched in fascinated horror as it turned, slithered past my feet and through the open door, across the veranda and then disappeared.

Gordon worked at the school for five terms, more than a year and a half, except for school holiday times though he sometimes went all the way there to check on the stock even then. Towards the end of this period I was becoming more and more troubled about what I observed in his inappropriate behavior around a young auxiliary who also worked there.

This unsavory situation continued despite the presence of her husband and in the face of my challenging him. My suspicions had been confirmed when she visited Lusaka and stayed in our home overnight. I was angry and hurt by her somewhat mocking attitude and malicious wit. Though bewildered by his attitude, I prayed for wisdom and calm. When our personal confrontation took place, he was all contrition, pledging reform, asking for forgiveness. His time at the school was almost over and I wanted to re-establish a stable relationship. Though very disappointed and heartsick, I made the decision, as a Christian, to forgive and asked God to help me. I trusted in His power to make that forgiveness real and in time He did just that. But a fatal flaw had been exposed and it was to bear bitter fruit.

In the following months, as my acute disappointment gradually yielded to the awareness of God's faithfulness in helping me, there were times when doubts and misgivings would cloud my consciousness, but I kept coming back to God's promises. As my hands and feet went from task to task, my mind was continually engrossed in a kind of dialogue. I mentally argued between introspection and the realities surrounding me, between what I read in the scriptures and their application to my personal situation, between the theory and the gut wrenching determination to put faith to work and be as loving and natural as possible. Even on difficult days, knowing something of my God, something of His power and compassion, I knew deep down I was compelled to keep going and not give up.

So through those uneven days, whether bone weary from labor, or occasionally heartened by hope, I constantly meditated on His word and gradually was able to focus more clearly on what I should be doing. The words lay on the page under my hand, but it was as if they spoke aloud. I must run with as good a heart, with as much determination as I could muster, the race that was set before me. That was the point it seemed. The race was mine to run, to endure and to win. The finishing line was far out of sight, yet unseen witnesses would cheer me on. I sensed the battle hardly begun, but I knew what I was fighting for, and I knew who had won the war. Not willing to give up, I decided to keep going.

Chapter 7
The Gray House

It was a gray day. Until well after lunchtime rain had fallen from a dull sky, and the cloudy dampness suited my mood. By late afternoon I was tired and fed up. Work and the financial struggle were getting me down. By teatime, the rain had stopped but still every leaf dripped and the grass underfoot oozed. I went outside just to feel the air and catch the faint breeze that often came just before sundown. Looking towards the river to the west of the house, there was just enough space between the departing clouds and the tree tops for the setting sun to send a few last rays of chartreuse light. Released from the house, the children gleefully ran about barefoot, stamping in the puddles on the road.

Driving the children home from school earlier, I was paying little attention to their bouncing and chattering until I caught the repeated phrase, "…the gray house." Suddenly I focused on what they were saying. The "gray house" was our new house, the one we were striving so hard to finish. Now I took a little time to look at it through their eyes. Grateful that at least we had adequate shelter and the promise of better things to come I had been too busy to bother with details. Now I saw it as they did.

What I saw was gray. We had built in concrete block with a cement plaster finish. The floors though smooth as silk not yet stained and polished, were also concrete gray. We had not yet painted the second-hand window frames.

Before I slept that night, I made a note at the foot of my list for the following day "Think color, think paint". And so an interesting pile of tins and new tools found their way into the shed, all ready for the weekend. On Saturday morning I revealed this treasure and produced pink, green and white paint, brushes and rollers. When the children realized what was afoot, their excitement knew no bounds. With me, they sloshed paint around with great abandon and by bed time the inside of the house was transformed. There was a fair amount of paint on the children too but they did not mind even when it proved hard to scrub off. Nothing could dampen their spirits. A few days later I bought yards of bright cotton material and made curtains and covers for their room.

The heavy work on the house and garden now took a back seat. Early in 1969 my mother-in-law, en route from Australia to England, broke her journey for a visit. She was the first family member to come. Gordon drove down to Durban to collect her and the following Friday I took the children down as far as the Victoria Falls to meet them so we could spend the weekend sightseeing. The children loved this trip and happily chanted all the way, singing a jingle they had made up:

"We're going on safari,
In the middle of Central Africa-
You wouldn't have thought, would you now?
Tra-la, tra-la, tra-la."

It became the family ' holiday' song and featured in every trip we took from then on.

Nana Bland was very active with auburn hair and was a whole new experience for the children. She ran and played, chased balls and swung on their homemade swing. When my mother visited later that same year, she was very different. This Grandma was plump with curly white hair. She knitted and told stories, so the children had the best of both worlds.

The two visits were coordinated, so that when I drove Nana Bland to her ship at Cape Town, I then waited a couple of days, had the car fully serviced and met my mother. She flew there for this very purpose, so I could give her the trip back up through South Africa. The long journey up country was a great opportunity for us both to relax and catch up on all the family news. She was a great letter writer and recorded her trip for the family and friends back in England. Taking the "Garden route" that is taking the coast road round the Cape from Cape Town to Durban was particularly enjoyable. Then we turned inland to the high veldt, via Johannesburg and then north. She vividly remembered driving through the Transkei in a very thick mist with me dodging the sheep that so often wandered on to the fenceless, winding road.

Both mothers gallantly coped with the incomplete house. At this time there was no hot water or electricity and only basic plumbing. During my mother's visit I was stricken again with severe back pain and was forced to take to my bed. She did very well with lamps and candles. It was not ideal but when faced with their proposed visits, we did not think we should put them off until it was more convenient. We were only conscious of the opportunities passing especially after the death of my father.

However, in point of fact, both visits went off well. On a trip through the Zambezi Valley we came across an elephant standing in the middle of the road. Nana Bland was sitting in the front and, as Gordon drew the car to a halt, she frantically rolled her window up tight. At the same time she pressed further and further back in her seat. Even while we sweated it out, I could not help smiling at her instinctive action. When the beast finally lumbered off, Gordon relaxed with a sigh. He had been poised to slam the car in reverse the whole time. We had recently seen a new Mercedes-Benz with a crushed hood where an irritable elephant had sat down. My mother extended her visit. She bought a load of local stone so our builder could put in a good fireplace in our sitting room and she helped establish a rose garden. Later I took her and the children on another sightseeing trip in the school holidays. While we were away Gordon stripped off the last of the old thatch and supervised the erection of a new roof.

The new roof was of corrugated asbestos, easily obtainable in Zambia where it was manufactured. At last the house looked better and was cooler than if we had used corrugated iron as was common. The pale gray roof quite quickly weathered to a pleasing shade that blended in with our trees. It was wide, low house with a patio facing the river. At first it had a door on the roadside, but after one memorable day when heavy rain broke a neighbors dam wall, which was built on higher ground, the escaping water flooded down the road and dumped more than an inch of muddy water throughout our house. We decided to block that door up, so both entrances were located at the back. These doors, one from the sitting room and one from the kitchen led to an expanse of rough lawn. Later this would be paved and become our main entertaining area. The stable doors gave lots of fresh air while ostensibly keeping dogs out and children in.

So life went on in a more colorful way. My back was troublesome at times, but we forged ahead. The children were healthy. The water rights on the river were granted. The remaining extent was purchased. Now that we held the land on both sides of the river we thought about its possible use. Across the river, the land opposite our house rose in a series of natural tiers and we thought it would make an excellent site for building some day. We were now able to get Electric power lines on to our land. This was our biggest investment yet.

Bringing the power lines to our land in order to get mains electricity to pump water and put lights in the house was a huge step forward. It was a costly investment but it also opened up the way for irrigation equipment. This was followed by the purchase of more dairy cows and a second-hand tractor.

Gordon found a job with an agricultural engineering firm, which was at least an 8am. - 5pm. Monday to Friday set-up. But it was not to last. He was not content and left barely a year later.

Meanwhile, another facet was about to be added to life on our small farm. This time it was something quite new, and we had no idea it was destined to point the way forward to our future ministry.

On day, a beaten up Land Rover limped into the drive with a punctured tire. The young married people were hot, and disheveled, that being their second puncture before the first could be repaired. They spoke of someone vaguely known to Gordon, from whom they had obtained directions to our farm. After refreshments and some general talk, we learned they were newly married and the young man had recently lost his job through injury in a mining accident and they had no place to go. They hoped Gordon might be able to suggest a possible source of work. Though a bit surprised, his special talent of being interested in people put them at ease and the couple was invited to stay, which they happily did in a very old tent.

Over the next few days, the tires got mended; the young couple felt more rested and a rapport among all of us well established. When Gordon suggested a certain connection in the game hunting area of the Luangwa Valley and later arranged an introduction to an established hunter, it proved to be exactly what suited. Jake became a successful hunter and spent many years working in the Safari business. What was more important, during this time with us, Jake and his wife became believers in the Christian faith and their lives were changed forever.

Gradually, a new way of living crept upon us. At first it was more an extension of how we had always been. Then, as the trend continued and we began to see a pattern emerging, we were forced to pause to consider, prayerfully, all the implications, to think through our response.

While Gordon and I were on exactly the same wavelength when it came to the use of our home and resources, and our hopes for the spiritual future of the whole place, he was already finding other opportunities. He became involved in the Gideons taking the Bible into hotels, the prison and to students. Since the mission school days, he had also been interested in the whole concept of teaching agriculture in the schools. This brought him into contact with V.S.O (Voluntary Service Overseas) youngsters and others - it was these activities that later brought Hal into our lives. Gordon was a founder member of ZEGEDA, the Zambian Agricultural Education Association. While I was kept busy assisting in many tasks that all this brought my way, together with continuing to rebuild our livelihood and home, nevertheless, I also became more and more conscious of people in need around us. It was as if God was bringing them into sharp focus.

In the multicultural mix that was Zambia, there were so many people outside the reach of the established churches and missions. There were lonely women in town and on farms; poverty stricken 'poor whites' living in the derelict caravan park outside the city; travelers and visitors who constantly passed through, especially young people who traveled unconventionally, often getting into trouble, ill, robbed or stranded; visitors who landed in the hospital or jail; and refugees. Many Mission and other Christian workers in lonely situations who needed a place to rest on occasion.

How would we know which of these to reach out to? Meeting special needs would take time, energy and stamina. Without an anointing for a ministry such as this, and the enabling of the Holy Spirit, it would not be possible. How wonderful to wait upon God to see how this could come about, to learn to be sensitive to the fact that He would choose the people and the circumstances, He would bring the people to us.

All through the early years in Bulawayo, Kitwe, and Lusaka, we had enjoyed and been part of a loose interdenominational fellowship of other missionaries, all of us being fully occupied with our own particular missions. Any time in fellowship with others of our own culture was sweet, but after our fire and as the children grew, we were very conscious of our need of a church home where we could settle. In short we needed building up before we could ever hope to continue a life of giving out again. We also knew we needed a church, for our own stability, and where we could confidently bring others in.

Our chosen church was fully able to fulfill those needs. At this time the ministry there was growing in leaps and bounds attracting a large number of students from the university and other colleges.

As civil war had raged through Angola and Mozambique for years, all North/South traffic in Africa out of necessity came through Lusaka. Now we were about to see some of the ways even this circumstance would yield a harvest for the Kingdom of God.

A friend came to tea one day, with her mother who was on a visit from South Africa. The mother's name was Queenie, a lady of deep faith and joyous nature. The ladies were shown around and then we all went back to the house.

The talk turned naturally to the various aspects of the farm and our hope for the spiritual work. The visitors expressed real interest in all that we shared. They were sympathetic when told about the long struggle to build the house. Suddenly, Queenie threw up her hands and started to pray. Not being used to her ways, we were a bit startled but quickly recognized the genuineness of her actions and listened intently.

Gesturing round the unfinished room, she prophesied that the day would come, in the not too distant future, when it would be filled with people praising God.

Her speech ended as abruptly as she had begun. There was complete silence in the room. For a few moments she remained standing, her eyes lifted up as if she saw into another dimension. Then in a second she laughed joyously and clapped her hands.

"My dears, believe it and prepare!" The spell was broken and everyone spoke together. The mood of expectation and encouragement was electric.

True enough, in the next few months, several more people found their way to our door and a pattern seemed to emerge. From time to time, some body would arrive, seemingly out of the blue showing unmistakable signs of need. We did what we could, though often it was not in the way of material things. We sought opportunities to speak to them about Christ whilst not putting on any pressure, and we endeavored to respond as the Spirit led. Sooner or later our visitor went on their way. But before long we were opening our door to yet another new face.

Added to these visitors were a growing number of young volunteers and students, from contacts in Zageda and the churches in town. That year the farm became a home-from-home for several young people who popped in on weekends and public holidays, all eager for fellowship and ready to lend a hand with whatever needed to be done.

This small but steady trickle of visitors was no problem. Indeed we were happy to see people and took it all in our stride. By this time we had acquired a few extra cheap iron bed frames for which I made mattresses from hay filled sacks. It was a long time before we graduated to three-inch deep foam. Each bed had one set of sheets, one pillow and one cheap locally manufactured blanket, plus a bright cotton cover. That was it. Our floors were polished concrete, stained dark with old engine oil and we had no carpets, just locally made grass mats in the bedrooms. It was all extremely unpretentious. There was still no hot water on tap and no indoor toilet. To ease pressure on the bathroom, male visitors were given a bar of soap and a towel and laughingly waved toward the river, "the shower is that way!"

Family life dictated the framework of our days. Despite the distance, we chose to keep our children at home in day school in Lusaka. This meant twice daily, later three times round trips of approximately twenty-five miles starting at 6.50am, completely dominating my time. However, everyone pitched in and contributed in some way. Our farming enterprise gave us plenty of plain fresh food. Many spiritual lessons were learned while weeding or churning butter.

Now the day came when we were forced to sit down and seriously consider where all this was leading. Should we seek to curtail the flow or continue to operate an open house? What was really happening? Was it just the result of our being friendly, helpful, and rather open-handed, or was it something more serious that God wanted and would use and bless? Was it what He intended for us all along? Indeed, since it closely involved our family way of life, we needed to be sure. We were aware that wisdom and discipline would be needed if we allowed this trend to continue.

We prayerfully considered every angle. Was our original intention that this small valley be used primarily for God's purposes about to come true? Could we really embrace a long-term lifestyle of sharing with other people? Could we truly know who was to benefit? Were there things we should specifically seek to do, or was it just that we continue to live and work, seeking only to be sensitive to the needs as they were presented and trust God to guide us in our response?

Chapter 8
Kusanga

We drove out of the farm drive and headed due west. We passed the Satellite Station, that symbol of 20th century progress and turned our faces towards a taste of the Old Africa. At least as much of that as remained. Even the remote bush sported Coca-Cola signs, and every now and again, we saw the hideous remains of a ghastly accident or the end of a dream of western style riches.

School was out and we were on our way to do our favorite thing, spend a few days relaxing in the bush. It was a good road and we kept the binoculars ready to hand. The two hundred- mile long journey was punctuated with glimpses of the wild. The children giggled to see a family of warthogs running in a line with their tasseled tails held erect like miniature flagpoles. A Secretary bird stalked through the tawny gray winter grass, and far off we saw the smoke rising from a bush fire. We started up a small herd of impala antelope and they bounded gracefully away. A single large tree standing on the roadside threw a patch of shade towards the road and we gratefully stopped for lunch.

There was no sound except the rustle and creak of the bush. A Lilac-breasted Roller alighted on a nearby bush and then we heard the distant clank of a tin can cowbell as some native cattle ambled our way. Turning round, we could see through the dry, winter thin grass the approaching group. Some young boys with their catapults in hand were calling to each other as they traditionally minded the village cattle. They amused themselves by hunting *kanyoni,* the prolific small bush birds. Occasionally the thrum of a passing vehicle with its canvas water bag hung on the front, would interrupt the quiet.

We followed the road as it dropped to the Kafue River and came to Iteshi-Teshi late in the afternoon. The air at that time of day was significantly cooler, for it was August and the winter barely over. The children scrambled out of the car and followed us as we clambered up on the huge rocks that were a common feature of the lakeside. The lake spread before us, wide, cool and deep, a sight for sore eyes. A thin dark line between the water and the sky delineated the far shore.

We returned to car, piled all our stuff in the chalet, and decided to stretch our legs before nightfall. Baboons trooped across the sandy track ahead of us, and on the evening breeze we caught the distant sound of African drums. The sun set in an amber blaze and in the brief tropical dusk we turned and made

69

our way back to camp. Hid deep in the bushes under our window, a Heuglin's Robin sang a sweet benediction. We ate watching the stars in the clear, dry season sky that seemed to bring them so close. When the moon rose it sent slivers of light slanting across the black water where the lake gleamed with a sleek, anthracite sheen.

After two days at Iteshi-Teshi, we made our way south through the Kafue National Park. Intrigued and enchanted as always, we came upon one delight after another. A giraffe, slowly straddling his fore feet wide in order to bend down to drink, a lone bull elephant sedately ambling along with three egrets perched in a line on his prominent spine. We came across zebra and wildebeest grazing together. The wildebeest is the clown of the bush, grunting, snorting, and sometimes skipping in an idiotic manner. With his lugubrious bearded face and top-heavy look, the wildebeest always looks odd especially when running with typical rocking motion. We caught sight of some sable antelope and when we stopped the car at one point, we realized a stately kudu bull was standing looking at us and poised for flight.

Huddled in our jackets in the dawn chill, we left the camp one morning and drove slowly, expecting something round every curve of the sand track. Suddenly, Stuart clutched my shoulder and I, in turn, touched Gordon's arm. He cut the engine and we silently rolled to a stop. We saw a male lion walking through the grass. His head with its great mane was held low, swaying from side to side slightly in time with his rhythmic gait. We watched with bated breath as he disappeared in the dense thicket several hundred yards away. We remembered to breathe and sat whispering and waiting to see if there were any other lions about. As the sun rose above the thicket, we saw three females following on in the same direction, silently walking in single file along a narrow path not far from the car. The last lioness had two cubs at her heels. No doubt she was training them, but whatever the reason, she led them to a bush in plain sight and bade them stay there. She followed the others and disappeared. Bidding the children not to make a sound, I rolled the car window down.

The cubs were in plain sight. They sat obediently for a bit, started to fidget and finally began to play. One chased a butterfly, his sibling followed. They tumbled and gamboled and gradually moved quite a way from the bush and nearer to our car. We were so enthralled we did not notice the lioness return. There was no sign of the others. Taking no notice of us, she coughed a recall to the cubs and they immediately ran her side. To our delight she sat down in front of us. The early sunlight behind her gave her tawny gold fur a luminosity and halo. The cubs climbed all over her, patting her muzzle and pulling her tail. Deep in her throat she began to purr. When the lioness got up and padded off, she called her cubs to follow, while we sat pinned to our seats with delight.

Continuing south, we kept to the track for the most part. Through the tall brittle grass in a sparsely wooded area we were tempted to leave the track and creep close to a family of giraffe. They did not run but viewed us, from over the low trees, with gentle eyes as if the game viewing was the other way round. A flock of hundreds of small birds rose and swirled, settled and rose again in the thorn bushes. The sun-baked savanna stretched before us, only inhabited by a large group of sable antelope. We saw their majestic curved horns and dark backs clearly against the ochre background as they stood up to their white bellies in the *dambo*. Gordon took the car off the road and we bumped over tussocks of coarse grass to take a closer look.

We pushed on south and finally left the Park in the direction of Kalomo. Next day we took the road to Livingstone and traveled the extra seven miles to the Victoria Falls. We saw the spray cloud that rises from "Mosi-o-tunya" (the smoke that thunders), several miles away. On a previous trip, very early in the morning we had seen the sunrise tinge this cloud salmon pink and so great are the mighty falls that as one draws nearer, the very ground trembles. Now the vast plume of mist spray was shot through with a double rainbow in the bright morning sun as the Zambezi River a mile and a half wide, plunged into the chasm more than three hundred and fifty feet below.

Next morning we drove back to Livingstone and followed the Zambezi River to Kazungula and the pontoon. There was little traffic and we made good time on the dirt road, the dust cloud kicked up by our wheels poured out behind us. We passed a couple, walking one behind the other, miles from any sign of habitation. The man stepped out in front just carrying his stick, the woman several paces behind with her baby tied on her back with a *chitenge* cloth. Her *katundu* was piled up in a shallow wide enamel bowl balanced on her head and she was knitting as she walked.

The vegetation was changing. Here and there huge baobab trees stood out along the roadside. An eagle soared into the air carrying a snake in its talons and up ahead a dust devil crossed the road swirling twigs and leaves and gravel into the air. The bush at the side of the road was coated with dust from the passing vehicles. We dropped down to the river and drew up at the pontoon. Getting out of the car to stretch our legs, we waited for the pontoon to return from across the river.

The ferrymen chanted as they hauled on the lines that linked the pontoon from one side of the river to the other. When the ferry docked, we watched folk get off with bundles and bicycles, then the children and I took our places on the ferry with a few other pedestrians, while Gordon carefully inched our car down the ramp and onto the ferry. Out on the water, we could see hippo bobbing in the water up to their pinkish knobby eyes. Occasionally they would yawn or snort and their twitching ears flicked spray in the sunlight.

We drove off the pontoon into Botswana. Here at the confluence of the Chobe River the borders of four countries came together, Zambia, Botswana, South West Africa and S. Rhodesia. That night at Chobe Camp, we sat watching the sunset over the mighty river. We listened to the hippos' deep grunting and the yelping cries of the fish eagles settling for the night. It was the quintessence of Africa and for a brief hour it was possible to forget the tumult of this rapidly changing continent.

The following morning found us out early to explore deeper into the reserve. The bush was hushed. Only the sound of our car engine disturbed the quietness. When we stopped and switched off the motor, the only sounds were of somnolent insects, the liquid call of a Laughing Dove and the occasional boom of a Trumpeter Hornbill deep in the bush.

The river stretched out before us. From our vantage on the lower river road we saw a large herd of elephant with young, spread out among the papyrus and swamp grass. The hot morning sun glinted off the water. Overhead a lappet-faced vulture circled on the lookout. A fish eagle's yelping call, *"Kow, kow, kowkowkow,"* rang across the water. He was perched on a dead tree stump, high above the river. We turned from watching a dug out canoe go by to find the elephant herd moving away upstream. Cautiously we followed, keeping a good distance back, driving round the cracks and holes in the dried mud road.

There were sometimes long distances between treats, but we did not mind. We expected something exciting round every corner. At one point we stopped the car to get out briefly, stretching and generally rearranging ourselves. At first we saw no game nearby. Then to my horror, I realized there were three elephants only about forty yards away. How amazing that such huge creatures should blend so well into the gray - ochre bush. Only the slow movement of their ears gave them away. They seemed to pay us no attention, but my heart was in my mouth as I bundled the children back into the car and hissed to Gordon to "get going, please."

All too soon it was time to go home. As we came through customs and crossed the river again, we felt relaxed and rested. The children agreed, it had been a great trip. We headed north, the road steadily rising. When we came to one of the tsetse barriers that guarded the high country from the danger of tsetse fly borne disease, our car was directed off the road into a large shed and thoroughly sprayed. Then we were free to take the road that followed the line of rail up to Lusaka.

Chapter 9
This Business of Loving Others

The way ahead became clearer when, a friend of ours from Nyasaland (now independent Malawi) arrived to stay with us overnight. He was driving an American Evangelist and his wife to the Copperbelt via Lusaka. As we finished breakfast the following morning, our friend went out to take their suitcases to the car, but the American couple hung back. They said they want to pray for me, and laying hands on me, they quoted Isaiah 58 v 10 & 11 which says-

"And if you spend yourselves on behalf of the hungry, and satisfy the needs of the oppressed, then your light will rise in the darkness and your night will become like the noonday. The Lord will guide you always; He will satisfy your needs in a sun-scorched land and will strengthen your frame. You will be like a well-watered garden like a spring whose waters never fail." They drew the parallel, that if I would be faithful in accepting and caring for those who came to our always open door, not neglecting to show them Christ, the Holy Spirit would give the increase. It was only after they had gone that I questioned in my mind why they had not included Gordon.

This was particularly encouraging, as we had not told any of them about how God was leading us in this respect. And so now we decided on a policy: We would not seek to attract people to the farm ourselves, only to respond to any need laid across our path, to accept those who arrived at our door with unsentimental love, as God gave us grace. To offer practical help if we could, good food, comfort, and friendship. Also to avoid the pressure of time it would be open ended - in other words, a place made available in our unique situation where there was time and opportunity to consider Christ and allow him to work.

These guidelines governing the various situations that ultimately faced us were very important, because they allowed us a freedom and confidence in our response. As the flow of people increased, the need to provide more accommodation became pressing. Thought was given to how the household would run and a Code of Discipline worked out.

The first of a group of small, very simple guesthouses was built in the grounds and some of the visitors helped with this. Their various skills were utilized to the full. In our early days, we had found a small spring in a hollow a little distance from the river. We felled a few small trees and cleared the bush with the idea of creating fishponds to add to our self-sufficiency, but it was not successful. At the height of the rains the flood from the river swept the walls away. Some time later, the outer walls was built up again and planted with weeping bottlebrush and willow trees. Carefully, we looked after these, having dug a deep ditch between the wall and the river to carry the excess water. Bulrushes and blue water lilies were established and in time the pool attracted additional wild bird life. We put one willow tree on a small island in the middle of the pool with nesting boxes, but it was difficult to keep the farm's ducks and geese there because predators were a constant problem. Nevertheless, the area was very lovely.

The civet and the genet are among the most common small predators. They are nocturnal and the genet particularly, is adept at climbing. From time to time, the farm poultry pens are raided and down on the pond it was even easier to lose domestic birds. One orphaned set of ducklings adopted a visiting hitchhiker as a foster-father. He took over the job of feeding them near the house and soon wherever he went, they followed at his heels. He said he was tempted to take them when he left, if only he could train them to fly over the customs post at Chirundu on the Zambezi River. We reckoned it was more a matter of teaching them where to land! Besides the crocodiles and lions on the opposite riverbank, the road was more hazardous. Border officials have big cooking pots.

Towards the river, beside the small spring, an early farm shed was converted into a thatched hut to sleep the overflow of visitors. It grew a bit, evolved a little and finally, in response to the need of a friend, it was improved to full cottage status with a bathroom, kitchen, solid roof and separate bedroom. It became "The Boathouse" which later was our family size guesthouse.

The downstairs guestroom of the old destroyed house was restored and a solar heater installed on the new roof. The French doors opened directly onto the lawns overlooking the river. Other small rooms sprang up built of all sorts of available odds and ends. For years I wished for more bathrooms, but as time went on, it became very evident that shortage of cash to build these was no hindrance to the Holy Spirit. The guestrooms were scattered about the grounds, each with it's own character, color scheme and name. A lot of prayerful though was given to these, for though we all ate together, shared the work and gathered for many activities, we were convinced privacy was important.

The dining room was not very big and just held a table seating twelve people, fourteen at a pinch. We could squeeze another eight places on other tables, but larger groups would be accommodated outside where there were several tables on the patio. Meal times were generally quite jolly times of animated conversation over plentiful home produced fare. Usually our own children sat my end of the table. On one memorable evening, under the cover of the hubbub, I rather sharply told them to take their elbows off the table. There was a moment's absolute silence, as nine other people stopped talking as though suddenly switched off, and nine other pairs of elbows were guiltily lowered.

As each small room was built as necessity dictated, I searched the second-hand furniture mart in town for likely pieces. Sometimes we heard of the contents of a house for sale or we would receive a gift. Mostly, I renovated, polished and sewed until each room was complete with comfortable beds, pretty curtains and covers, a desk, a bookshelf with books for relaxation as well as those providing good Christian reading, rugs, towel rack and a good chair, together with clothes space, bedside table and lamp. It was my custom to provide all rooms with fresh flowers and to pray in the rooms for those who would come.

In the early days, after a guest had left, the room would be cleaned and left, only being put ready again when someone arrived. Learning through emergencies, late arrivals and unexpected needs this way of doing things was soon reversed. No sooner was room vacated and cleaned; it was prepared again. Finally, I went to it to pray, taking flowers. These were renewed every few days whether the rooms were empty or occupied. The first man to actually thank me for this small service that spoke of its message of peace, beauty and welcome and what it meant to him, was a Vietnam War veteran from America who had arrived in a very exhausted and distressed state.

In time several simple rooms grew up around our farm-house. "The Boathouse" had porthole shaped windows; "The Hut", a small thatched and whitewashed converted shed was covered in bougainvillaea, near a huge jacaranda tree. "The Beehive", which we built with curved roofing sheets, kindly donated by a friend, resembled a dome and was flanked by frangipani bushes; "The Cabin" with a simple open veranda overlooking a big prickly pear clump. The "Cottage" overlooked the fields and was half hidden amid lemon trees and coral creeper, while the ivy clad "Ivy Room" and the "Garden Room" both, were parts of the old house restored, alongside the old kitchen, which was made into a room to house our book and tape library.

The back of the kitchen door served as our "notice board." School routine and farm work shaped our days. Everyone was invited to go with the family on Sundays to the church in town and to join any other gatherings for worship, prayer and fellowship on the farm but no pressure was put on folk. In every room there was a copy of our Code of Discipline covering behavior, use of telephone and transport, and also the visitors' boundaries in relationship to our children, our belongings and our staff. Many of our visitors had never lived in a structured Christian home but this, in itself, led to many talks and opportunities to present to Gospel.

All that we could offer was available for three days. After that, any visitor wishing or needing to stay had to come and discuss their reasons for doing so, so that except for cases of illness, arrangements could be made whereby the visitor made a contribution towards their keep. Everyone had to look after their own room, share in basic chores and do their own laundry in a large shed we had fitted out for that purpose away from the house. We were always available to talk and one evening each week was given over to music, prayer and study.

The kitchen was the hub of the house. The east window overlooked the drive, so I was always aware of the movement of vehicles and visitors. The back door opened onto the patio, which ran the length of the house, and through it one could see all the way down the river. Countless meals were cooked getting to know people and many a late drink was shared round its central table as serious inquirers delved into the life of faith and grew in understanding.

The kitchen light was the last to go off in the shared part of the house, and the first to come on in the morning, when the doorbell rang to signal the watchman going off duty. The farm keys would be handed out, then with distant clink and clatter from the dairy borne on the fresh morning breeze, I would sit on the step with a mug of tea and some bread to hand feed my peacock. A precious time slot before being overtaken by the bustle of the day.

The peacock, whose unheralded appearance at the farm was a source of great delight to me, had quickly established his own routine. Not everyone appreciated his raucous cries, but I rather liked to hear his ringing call punctuating the day. His routine rarely varied. From his early meeting with me, he walked up the farm lane, had a cursory peck round the stock feed shed, strutted round the farm office building and paraded on the roof. A little later he would disappear into the woodland beyond the dairy. He reappeared from the direction of the waterfall in the late afternoon, displayed himself up and down the lawn, pecked about under the hibiscus hedge, and finally took a potter through the rose garden to complete his day.

Occasionally the peacock would stroll by the turkey pens and unsuccessfully try to interest them in his proud display. Often, after rain, he would hop up on the high archway in the garden wall and drape his tail in a resplendent fan to dry against warm brickwork. Wherever he spent his nights remained a mystery but he invariably turned up at the kitchen door at the sound of the bell in the morning.

Although our hearts went out to those in obvious need, it was a concern in the early days about how well we could communicate with people of very different backgrounds. For myself, the Lord confirmed his calling by anointing me with the gift of hospitality, the ability to discern needs before they were spoken and an instant loving acceptance of all who came whatever they were like. After all, as we learn from scripture Jesus always met people where they were at, people do not change until after the experience of an encounter with Him. Most people did not take advantage of us in the freedom available while we had trusted God with the risk of being 'ripped off' from the start.

The many and diverse ways people found their way to us never ceased to interest us enormously, indeed many times we heard the stories and were struck with awe. Arrivals happened at all hours, in many different circumstances and from many causes. Situated barely eleven miles west of the city center on a country road, we considered ourselves off the beaten track. We were to learn the beaten track ran right past our door. Extraordinary things were shared with strangers, though most people did not remain strangers long.

One of the earliest incidents was shared with a local lad staying with us briefly before the farm was fully built. At this time Gordon and I were temporarily sleeping in the hastily repaired kitchen of the old house, while the builder worked on our bedroom. I woke up after an awful nightmare of being pursued by a ghostly dog. In the dream, every time I had attempted to catch it, this enormous pale mauve fluffy animal evaporated, only to appear again and again to threaten us. Time after time, when I put my hand out it would pass clean through the dog. Still feeling shaky, I got up and went to the door. It was dawn and I stood on the doorstep and looked over the lawn, and saw a strange dog facing me, cowering and frothing at the mouth. I guessed it was rabid. At that moment the door of the new house opened and one of the children appeared and let our own dog out.

Shouting to the child to get back in and shut the door fast, I called my husband urgently. Our dog went for the strange one, which slunk into some nearby bushes, where our dog baited it, cornered it against the fence and they fought. Our young visitor appeared and attempted to catch our animal, with me screaming, "Do be careful", very aware of the danger. Finally, our furiously barking dog was coaxed off and shut in the house. The rabid dog, for such it was later proved to be by the government vet, finally slunk off and was later shot by a neighbor.

It was only when the family got together and took stock, that our probable danger became evident. Saliva from the rabid dog coated our dog's muzzle and neck and both visitor and children, who had scratches on knees and hands, had handled our dog in the excitement as they hauled it into the house.

Our doctor, when consulted, urged safety and advised the whole family and our guest to have rabies vaccinations, at that time a series of fourteen daily jabs placed in a circle round the navel. So we went off to get the free serum from the Chemist and then all duly lined up outside the doctor's room. Our young visitor gamely offered to go first "to show the kids there was really nothing to it". Minutes later, he reappeared at the door as white as a sheet.

"Nothing to it, kids." he quipped and hit the floor in a dead faint.

It was not that easy to take three small children day after day for injections because they stung. But Mum and Dad routed the party home via the toyshop and ice cream parlor on alternate days and we got through it. Still, there was one amusing sequel. The injection sites stung and soon itched like mad as the sequence built up over the fortnight. On the second Sunday, Gordon and I were both caught standing on the church steps talking to our friends, both unconsciously scratching away at our stomachs.

As our workload increased, in building as well as farm work, we added steadily to our staff. An amusing side to employing Zambians was their liking for several names; the family or Tribe name, childhood name, often a "nickname" and many then choose another name they like when they grow up. Often these names are of things they like; sometimes the childhood name sticks throughout their life. We had a "Thousand", a "Tickey" named after the Rhodesian name for the old English silver three penny bit, the exceptionally tall "Size", a "Scissors" and, my favorite name, "Ikwanira" our tractor driver. He was the youngest of a very large family so his mother nicknamed him "Ikwanira" that means, "That's enough!"

So we went on, sharing the mundane and the precious with an ever-increasing number of people who came from far and wide. There were many different stories about how they had arrived at the farm. Some felt it was by chance, others had deliberately taken the decision to come and others, seeing clearly in retrospect, the various connecting steps, sometimes over different continents, that they acknowledged to be God's hand on their life to bring them to a knowledge of Himself.

Chapter 10
The Open Gate

It was the era of hippie backpackers who roamed the world in search of adventure, knowledge, other cultures or who had just plain "dropped out." A good many traveled all over Africa, many on their way overland going on to sample the delights of India - or were on their way back. They came from all over the world, single, in pairs, groups, or on organized expeditions. Among them many ran into problems, being robbed, falling ill and a host of other tribulations. Among this throng were many that consciously or unconsciously were on a spiritual pilgrimage and God had his loving hand on so many. A fair number found their way to Yieldingtree Farm

It was evident to many, and even more so to us, that the hand of God played a definite part in bringing people to our door. Of course there was the natural way in which some travelers met others and passed the word on, yet God used this too. People were surprised to find the farm not quite what they expected. Whatever they said, a hidden need, or deeper purpose would often become evident. In this quiet backwater, they were faced with the challenge of the Gospel and had the time and opportunity to explore, learn, think and make their response. Some were merely the link to others.

Those who found God told tales of extraordinary contacts. One man was given our address jotted down and given to him on a boat in the Red Sea. A girl that became ill and stranded in hospital received our address from a local Christian nurse. An English student wrote of her experiences at the farm to a friend in Holland. A year later, she also came to a new understanding of Christ on the farm. When a motorist on a lonely dark road saw a hitchhiker caught in the blinding rain, he gave him a lift and brought him to our gate. Robbed and stranded, another traveler struggled to find shelter only to find assistance with an acquaintance of ours. He arrived the following day and stayed three months, a renewed man. One Lusaka businesswoman sent a traumatized and exhausted traveler to us in her own vehicle after he had collapsed in a lunch bar in the city

Meeting practical needs, even feeding people sometimes called for a bit of ingenuity. Very late one night, I nearly fell foul of our watchman's club. I had pulled on an old raincoat and crept into the kitchen garden by torch light for some salad stuff to eke out the scrambled eggs and bread which was all I had handy to offer a carload of people just then arrived. However, with

79

a mixed farm there was always something on hand and as the farm grew, both the livestock and the fruit trees, together with garden produce yielded an abundant harvest year round.

We knew nothing of LSD and similar drug substances but we soon learned. We were often faced with new situations among the somewhat freewheeling young visitors, quite outside our own experience, but discipline, compassion, practical assistance and humor, dispensed in various combinations went a long way towards keeping the balance. The other Christian residents on the farm also had a very valuable input, as did several friends visiting from distant Mission stations from time to time.

This wandering fraternity was not the only group to come. There was a sprinkle of refugees and a number of more local people in need. Among the V.S.O. (Voluntary Service Overseas) personnel we had met, there was one, an English girl who wanted to study tropical agriculture on her return to England. Before leaving she spent time on the farm and later we learned she had won a place at Seal Hayne Agriculture College in England. Gordon, through his interest in Z.A.G.E.D.A. (Zambia Agricultural Education Association), had a contact there. Subsequently this student was allowed to come out to the farm to do her practical 'sandwich' courses. Gordon arranged various study opportunities for her around the country together with research facilities. She did so well, and came top in her year. This opened the way for several other students to come from England in the next few years to do likewise. Students whose letters we prayed over beforehand. Some of them came to know Christ.

When I had sought the Lord about my own ministry years before, I felt I was being made to think about all the people in Zambia who were not Africans. There were very many British and Afrikaans of course, together with missionaries from many countries. There were also many professional people, some of whom spent their spare time and money on mission work. But alongside all of these, of which only a small minority made their way to the house of God, was vast number of people of many different nationalities living and working in Zambia. Polish and Greek families who had settled after World War ll, Portuguese, Italians, people from Romania and Yugoslavia who came with the big business consortiums to built Lusaka's International Airport, Kariba Dam and other projects; members of the Diplomatic Corps, German, American Japanese and many others.

It was therefore no great surprise that a percentage of all these people and others should at one time or another come into our orbit and often that led to spiritual opportunities. In one year alone, we had contact with nine Japanese visitors at the farm.

One very unusual opportunity occurred to give aid to a Russian lady and her child, to have them stay while they waited for diplomatic channels to clear the way for their repatriation. Another time a lovely North Korean girl with a housing problem was brought to the farm, but she was speedily whisked away in an Embassy car a week later - no doubt they were fearful of her being influenced by western Christians. She had so enjoyed those few days with us and wept as she secreted a New Testament in her pocket. Some weeks later, I saw her in the city, though not near enough to speak to. She waved and her eyes filled with tears as she was hustled away.

All this, while giving us fascinating glimpses into the richness and problems of other cultures, also prompted us to add books in several languages to our library whenever we had opportunity. Early on, the Christian Literature Crusade generously gave us a grant that we deeply appreciated. Time and again, we were thankful to be in a position to use or give out a Bible or guidance literature in a particular language so readily, for while many people had a good command of English, some did not. It was always preferable for them to study and search in their own mother tongue. To the library was also added a large collection of study and message cassettes from some of the world's leading expositors and teachers of the Christian faith and spare tape players were made available for visitors.

Devotional evenings were arranged each week. Music usually guitars accompanied songs and prayer, with Gordon, Hal and others taking a turn at leading. These were held informally in the sitting room of the farmhouse. Everyone staying on the farm was made welcome but no pressure was put on. Many a visitor who had said "no thanks" was later discovered sitting outside on the patio where everything could be heard through the open windows without them having to come in. At one particular period when there was a fairly large group wanting to learn, a teacher came out weekly from our church in town to hold a regular Bible Study.

There were often visits from missionary friends from many denominations, whether for short breaks or because they had to travel long distances to the capital for business. Several families came to stay periodically when they collected their incoming children from school overseas, or were sending them off. Often we wished we had more to offer in the way of comfort. Other visitors also greatly benefited from this additional ministry and those interested could learn a lot about the varied districts and the work that was done there by the various missions.

The principle that all who came to the farm, unless ill, could stay for only three free days, worked well. After that all visitors must contribute or work in some capacity. The three days gave travelers chance to rest up, do laundry, get money etc., and it also opened up an opportunity for them to taste Christian family life and hear the message. Many a time, someone that planned to go after the first three days, changed their mind and stayed. Some, of course, were forced to stay for a while by their circumstance, but God had his hand on it all. Everyone contributed, either at the building work at our outreach across the river, on the farm or in the house, where the work turned out to be therapeutic for many.

From New York came a woman who confessed she had never actually worked in a garden. She found a whole new enjoyment afterwards eating her teatime strawberries. She had learned how to weed them. A fishing trawler-hand from Scotland realized his boyhood ambition in learning to drive a tractor. Traumatized through loss and illness, a man found a renewal of peace working in the rose garden. An Australian TV producer, while seeking God and endeavoring to rebuild her life, found fun in helping to arrange a wedding reception. Others mended our cars, drove our children to, from school, tended our stock, and mended our fences.

Everyone enjoyed the contributions from the kitchen from Danish baking, Israeli and Greek cooking to a Swedish girl's artistry in icing a birthday cake. Some learned to churn butter, some grew vegetables and some sewed. Whatever was needed got done. The farm produced a very high percentage of our food requirements. Poultry for eggs and table birds, pigs and sheep for meat together with beef cattle. Dairy cows provided milk, cream, butter and cheese. The orchards and gardens provided a wide variety of fruits and vegetables year round. I made all the jams, preserves and pate.

As the number of people to be fed grew, so our efforts to be self-sufficient expanded. Most of our endeavors did very well. The exception was my experiment with turkeys. My rosy imagination had me providing economical suppers, holiday feasts and grand dinners, but my ideas soon bit the dust of reality. I had not reckoned on wild dogs, feral cats, marauding snakes, hawks and the turkey's own suicidal tendencies. In the end there was more entertainment than feasting to be enjoyed from the few survivors.

With some difficulty, fifty newly hatched turkey chicks were purchased. We put them to grow in a chicken brooder house with a batch of layer chicks. It was fascinating to watch them grow so fast. After only three weeks, they stood high above the chicks as if on stilts. But as the heat was reduced and the time came to introduce the flock to a cool growing shed it was the turkeys that objected. Fussy, they huddled and fiddled with their food. By the end of the first month, they just stood around, a desultory, scrawny bunch in amongst the sleek, happy chicks. Despite my efforts in separating them and putting them into a pleasant, shady outdoor run, they refused to co-operate and one by one just gave up the ghost until only a handful reached maturity.

Not willing to give up, we decided not to eat the remainder but try to breed from them. Accordingly, we gave some thought to their possible needs and made a much bigger pen, so they could have more natural environment. To my delight they did lay and sit. But we were not the only people observing them.

Thieves were perhaps to blame for whole clutches of eggs disappearing. The genets raided the chicks, then the adult birds. One morning only ripped wire and bloody scattered feathers remained. The great turkey experiment was over.

In the interests of self-sufficiency, we established a small flock of sheep, mainly for meat and trained a young local lad as shepherd. Now lambs were added to the farm. The children especially loved all of this. Birthday parties were easy. The children showed off the delights of the chicks, the calves, piglets and lambs and when they had seen the cows being milked, the tractor working and enjoyed a paddle in the river, it was time to come back to the house. We usually finished the day with homemade ice cream cranked in a barrel. No other entertainment was necessary.

Our young shepherd lad was very tall and his name was Size. One day helping out in the poultry houses, he suddenly cried out, fell over unconscious. His workmates ran to fetch me and I rushed up there but he seemed dead. I tried artificial respiration without success. Gordon was in town, so I fetched blankets and the men wrapped him and laid him in the back of the pickup truck.

As I drove to the hospital, over and above my shock, I wondered if he could have been electrocuted. We had installed all our own wiring in the poultry houses. Could it have been faulty? He had been working barefoot, carrying water to the chickens. Even his work mate jumped to the conclusion that "the electric had grabbed him" and had shouted this to another worker, who with great presence of mind, leapt to shut off the mains supply.

At the hospital Size was official declared dead and an autopsy ordered. He was only 21. When I returned to the farm, his family was already waiting, lined up outside our house, wailing and sobbing. It was awful. When Gordon returned he immediately checked on the wiring in the building where Size had fallen but could not find any fault. Two days later, the coroner's report told us this tall, gentle boy had died of a blood clot in his brain. Later we learnt from his family that he had suffered dizzy spells and had fallen over at home a few times immediately before his death. But this had not been observed in working hours.

Of course, the basic work of the farm was carried on with the regular paid staff, for this was our family's living and the farm business also financed all our other endeavors, but often it was very good for the visitors to work alongside the Zambians. Many visitors had skills that enormously helped things along, electricians, carpenters, builders and mechanics. There were painters, musicians, plumbers and cooks, all turning their hand to the task most needed, many to embark on a new spiritual life at the same time.

A great deal of maintenance of the house and guest rooms was done this way. In addition to their day-work, everyone cleaned their own room, did their own laundry and took turns with the washing-up. There was also plenty of time to talk with us. A lot of meals were taken outside on the patio, and there were barbecues, swimming in the river and film shows of all sorts. At Christmas time a carol service was held on the lawns with the neighborhood invited. There were three wedding receptions held in the garden, all arranged and catered for by our own combined talents.

Sometimes there were fishing trips and visits to the game parks arranged. Gordon, with his wide knowledge of African fauna and flora, always enjoyed taking these parties off the main road. Many of the old Rhodesian roads were 'strip roads'. That is twin narrow tar strips which despite the balancing act required, were nevertheless a great improvement over dirt tracks especially in the rains; then there were the nine feet wide tar strips that meant both vehicles driving with a set of wheels off the tar when they passed. Gradually over the years these old roads were fully tarred, but the fascination of going deep into the bush and seeing the game animals never diminished. The family also enjoyed many trips to the Victoria Falls in the school holidays.

Christmas was always a wonderful time and usually there were several other people gathered with the family to celebrate. On one memorable holiday, the children were given water pistols. However, the donor kept back a whole lot more, which he later gave out to many of the adults. The result was a total riot that threatened to drown the house.

Overland expedition tours, which plied between London and Johannesburg, found their way to Yieldingtree. These were usually converted Bedford trucks, fully self sufficient and carrying up to twenty people. The first driver to come sought us out with a request. Having met someone on the road that knew us, he drove out to the farm. Gordon, busy that morning in the cattle paddocks looked up when he heard the Bedford truck approach. The driver braked and looked down from the cab and called out.

"I'm looking for Gordon Bland."

"You've found him." Gordon left the paddock and the driver stepped down. He pushed his battered hat back and stepped forward to shake hands. Several faces peered down from under the rolled up canvas sides of the truck.

He spoke for a few moments and Gordon gestured toward the farmhouse. The driver climbed aboard and slowly drove down the drive with Gordon following.

I was at the kitchen window when the truck pulled up and Gordon called out for me to 'put the kettle on'. Telling the passengers they could swim in the river if they wished, Gordon ushered the driver round the patio. I took the tea tray out and sat down with them.

"I've had to leave one of my passengers in the hospital," the driver began.

"I'm sorry to hear that. Can we help?"

"Well, yes, if you would. It'd take a load off my mind, thanks"

"Right, tell us how," I joined in. The driver put us in the picture - the passenger, a young woman, was taken ill shortly after being robbed of her passport and money. She was likely to be in the hospital for about two weeks. The driver had to get his other passengers to Johannesburg and could not expect to return in time.

"Look, it's no problem," I spoke up. "I'll pop in and see her. She's welcome to come to us when she leaves the hospital and we'll take it from there." I looked across at Gordon for confirmation and he nodded."

"Don't worry. Come and see us when you return."

"Is it possible for us to camp here?" Asked the driver, looking around. "We've been using that old camp ground just south of town but it's pretty rough."

"Well, yes, I think so," Gordon looked thoughtful, then more emphatically, "Yes, do that. I'll show you where."

When the truck returned within the month, the young woman, restored to health, in possession of a new passport and with money sent out from her home, was eager to be on her way again. But by now she was seriously interested in the gospel of Christ. And so began another phase of the farm ministry.

Word spread among other drivers of that company and others. Soon there was regular traffic of this sort. A simple site was put at their disposal, with separate ablution block, under the spreading Cassia trees between the farmhouse and Sharon Cottage and these groups were welcomed to use everything the farm had to offer. Passengers spread their tents in the woods between the site and the river, so while they were self-sufficient, there was plenty of opportunity to mingle with the farm residents and they were always invited to whatever was going on. Over the years the interaction with these groups always brought interest, challenges and opportunities for service. Not surprisingly, here also was a harvest field in which God moved.

Chapter 11
The Yielding Tree

In all these busy years we had not been overseas to see our family since 1964. Now after ten years, I took an opportunity to go to England via Switzerland where I visited L'Abri to assist a friend who had been taken ill there. I stopped over in Germany to see Kris and his young lady. But although I benefited from this trip, the pain in my back was constant and soon after my return home I had to take to my bed again.

In 1975, after a particularly difficult and pain filled time with my old back injury, Gordon decided we should both go to England. Just beforehand, the leaders of our church in town came out to the farm specifically to pray for my healing but the problem remained.

By our departure date in October, I was exhausted. Deep down I could not reconcile the prognosis from my doctor that I was likely to be permanently crippled within a few years, with the vision I felt sure God had given me. Accordingly, I privately resolved to seek a Christian doctor in England with whom I could talk.

A young ex-teacher friend, son of a farmer, Hal had come to work for us as farm manager and with house and farm in competent hands, we set off. On arrival, we stayed with friends in Purley, London and on the first Sunday accompanied them to church. The pastor got up to pray and referring to their many people and missions usually prayed for, said "This time, ask God for one thing for yourself," so in a packed church, in pain and in faith, very simply I silently asked, "Lord, what about my back?"

There was no appreciable difference in my condition except some reduction in the pain. That was possibly due to me being in a position to rest more. Three weeks later I had found a dedicated Christian doctor and subsequently a specialist appointment was set up at Birmingham General Hospital. When the day came, the specialist was rather abrupt and tersely informed me there was nothing wrong. His manner even hinted at me wasting his time. A little dazed I walked down Corporation Street towards my bus and slowly the realization came to me that my back was healed. I was never to have so much as a backache again.

Though quietly thrilled and thanking God, I did not make a big thing of it to others at the time. Gordon was away visiting elsewhere and although I was now free of pain, I waited upon the test of time. Then something rather extraordinary happened. A week or so later, a letter arrived from the hospital in a brown 'window' envelope. When I opened it, it was in fact the consultant's follow-up letter to the doctor, confirming what he had said to me even down the chiding expression of his surprise I had even been sent in the first place.

If ever I was to have doubts, I now held proof positive in my hand. Over the telephone the doctor and I laughed and praised God as I explained that the letter had been folded incorrectly so that the patient's reference address, mine, was shown through the envelope's window, instead of hers. I happily promised to send it on.

The children were growing up and the following year plans were set in motion for Grace to go to college in England. Things were going well on the farm and someone came to us to act as housekeeper. Grace and I duly went off in September 1977. Indeed, my parting instructions to the temporary housekeeper had an amusing sequel. Reminding her not to forget to use the available fruit, especially the plentiful guavas, I was met on my return with doleful tales of guavas appearing in various guises at breakfast, lunch and supper for weeks. No one, it seemed, ever wanted to see another guava.

From the very early days of the farm's 'open gate', the wide variety of visitors had enriched the lives of those living at the farm. We had laughed and cried, believed and prayed together, labored and supported one another and many wonderful things happened. Not all our visitors were young and the years brought a miscellany of old and young, believers and nonbelievers, of different cultures and persuasions from all over the world. Whatever the ups and downs in our family or farm life, God's gracious Spirit was quietly at work changing lives, giving new direction to many. How some of these visitors ever heard of the farm or found their way to us was amazing.

To many, the farm was an unexpected oasis on their journey. In the early days of seeking God regarding our ministry, I had received a vision of Christ standing at our river with arms outstretched. Now we saw our lovely *manzi-amoyo*, water of life, being a great source of pleasure and beauty to many. Its *bilharzia* free spring water was safe, revitalizing body and spirit. Nothing more dangerous dwelt there than the tiny fresh water crabs which nibbled the toes and tickled the swimmers.

There were a few people early on in the ministry whose time at the farm was particularly significant, mainly because their association with Yieldingtree benefited the family long afterwards. Indeed some of these people either returned to work there or were especially supportive in their continued interest and friendship. Sometimes their experience was conveyed to others in writing or personal contact, and that naturally led to the farm becoming better known. But whatever natural ways contributed, many found their way in circumstances beyond their control, yet in their subsequent spiritual awaking, who could doubt God had his hand on every detail.

Mary came to Zambia first as a Canadian Volunteer, and returned later to do post graduate research. Although she had given up her search for God and had embraced the free-lifestyle in her North American University, nevertheless it was her testimony that during a stay at the farm God crept up on her bringing her to new faith and commitment. She later became a teacher in her field with a significant part to play in intellectual Christian circles.

Many times it was not possible to know how some people reacted to what they experienced while at the farm. All were accepted and loved and many sent on with our blessing. Our prayers followed them as we trusted the seed sown would ultimately bear good fruit. In England, my brother read in a travel book a long piece, which he recognized as being about Yieldingtree, clearly revealing the author's lasting impression. When my brother told us this, we remembered assisting the author one dark, rainy night beside the road. He was traveling the world on a motorcycle and came back to the house with us for two or three nights.

Leaving the Mkushi area, some two hundred miles from Lusaka, where we had been visiting friends, we gave a lift to a hitchhiker who waved us down. Close up he looked in very poor condition and once in the car it was clear he had a fever, so instead of dropping him off in town we brought him home. He was from Chile, and although Spanish was his language, his English was fair. Traveling overland on his own via East Africa, he had been robbed of all his money and things in Kenya. Making his way to Nairobi, he lived rough, sleeping out while waiting to get a new passport. Aiming to get down to South Africa and obtain work for money to go on, he made his way south. The poor living and scant food during that period had taken its toll and he became ill. We learnt he had responded to the gospel when young though had drifted since.

When he recovered he stayed on and offered his professional skills to lay the electric power lines across the river to our buildings there, where he also completed the wiring of all those buildings. It was a major contribution that saved us a lot of money. Not only that, in his spare time he demonstrated extraordinary skill at the sewing machine. Having received an anonymous cash gift he made new clothing, a tent and knapsack. When he left he was fully kited out with a Spanish Bible in his bag.

An American veteran soldier traveled with a group of Christians from Europe. This group had come down from Kenya. With them, he became stranded when their air-charter company went broke. A friend of ours met the group in Lusaka and brought them out to the farm. The American, who had but recently been freed from heroin addiction, was due to get married in Switzerland upon his return. Moreover he had recently come to faith in Christ. But he was considerably stressed by this unexpected setback in their plans.

I welcomed them in and offered drinks all round. Among the lively group, this one tired, thin young man stood out by reason of his dropping attitude. Anxious blue eyes looked up at me from a wan, bearded face. The hand that ineffectually pushed back his sweat-soaked hair trembled. Diffidently, he whispered a request for some water only, no coffee. Then he clasped his hands between his knees as if to still their tremor. As he talked we realized we knew his sweetheart's family. They lived in Zambia but some three hundred miles away.

We contacted them and, though they could not come then because of ill health, they arranged their daughter's flight from Switzerland and we planned the wedding at the farm. It was the first wedding to be held there. Two girls from Finland, in that same group, acted as bridesmaids. It was a much stronger and spiritually stable young man who took his bride back to the United States several weeks later.

An English teacher who had come to Lusaka on contract met Mac, a civil engineer, in the church there. Both had answered the call to get involved in our outreach across the river. Theirs was the second wedding at the farm and they remained friends and good supporters of the farm ministry for many years until they returned to Europe.

It was at breakfast one morning. One young man, who was stranded and waiting on God for the means to move on, was expressing his worry over a letter from home. A girl across the table quietly said, "I've got enough. Let's go into town and get you an air-ticket home." Within 48 hours he was on his way. What joy it was to see people moved into the hitherto unknown experience of spontaneous giving.

Hal, our farm manager, met the lovely Jo when he was taken ill and landed in Lusaka's Teaching Hospital where she was the nursing Sister on the casualty ward. In time, theirs was the third wedding on the farm but by no means the last romance. The families came out from England and everyone helped to make it a wonderful day. Rose, who was staying on the farm had been a trained cutter in London haute couture. After she and I searched Lusaka for suitable material, even at one point literally on hands and knees in a dusty warehouse matching lace, a stunning dress was designed and made by Rose. Of pearl gray silk, the dress was reminiscent of an 18th century gown with deep lace ruffles falling at the elbows. The back, falling to a half train at the back enhanced by tiny bows from neck to hem. Hal and Jo lived on the farm until late 1978 and were its staunchest co-workers and supporters.

Rose, in her 60th year, had written to us from Australia asking if she could stay with on her forthcoming trip to Zambia. She explained in her letter who had given her our name as a contact. We had no hesitation in bidding her welcome, thinking it would be for a few weeks only. Little did we guess that her visit would stretch and turn into an association lasting two and half years.

Of Swiss -German descent she was a lady of rare spiritual gifts who had come to give more than to receive. Though, untrained she had a heart and a burden for Zambia. She was able to get a work permit and despite difficulties with the vernacular language, completely gave herself in support of the local outreach, the farm ministry and the family.

From France came a young man touring the world with only a folding bicycle, two T-shirts and one spare set of socks and underwear. The bike folded down into a sturdy suitcase. Its owner was flying to various countries and using the bike for all his local travels once landed. His ingenuity was only matched by his laid-back personality and it seemed we made little impression on him. Even when no spiritual response seemed evident, we had learned that many times a visitor would afterwards prove to be a contact link for someone else. This turned out to be the case with our young cyclist.

It was not always easy to see people go off and not know what happened to them, but often there were those who stayed longer, getting close to the family who were able to share and rejoice in the changes wrought in their lives.

From Australia came two girls who had cycled vast distances through Africa. When circumstances brought them to the farm, all the guestrooms were full. A great effort was made to fit them in which they genuinely seemed to appreciate. After the customary three days, they felt more rested and asked if they could stay another week or so and "Could we use them?" One was a woodworker and one a plumber. Together they completely revamped a bathroom, fitting new vanity casing and cupboards. They also became a contact for someone else.

We had retired for the night when word was brought by the night watchman that people were at the gate needing help. They were nurses returning to a mission hospital far out to the west. Their vehicle had broken down on the main road near the end of our lane. The farm tractor, which had often turned out on similar occasions, was sent to tow their vehicle in while a couple of people from the farm went with the watchman with extra torches to guide the folk in. The farm was so full that night that several had to sleep on the sitting room floor.

One stormy evening after dark an overdue overland expedition truck sheered an axle a mile from the farm. It happened so suddenly, the huge Bedford truck lurched into a ditch and the eighteen passengers in the back were thrown about. The co-driver walked in to fetch help. Several cars from the farm set off to ferry passengers and their luggage back in the pouring rain. One passenger had hit his head so hard he was temporarily blinded. The driver stayed with the truck until our tractor arrived at first light to tow it in. The repairs necessitated waiting for spare parts to be flown from England. Meanwhile, the driver fell ill and was forced to stay on, so then there was a further delay as they had to wait for a replacement driver to be flown out from England. Fortunately the man with the badly bumped head recovered quickly. Two people on that expedition responded to Christ through all that.

At the approaching roar of a motorbike I opened the door in time to see a huge Triumph braking to a halt. The rider cut the engine and stepped down. As I took his hand in greeting, I felt the tremor. A lopsided smile did little to hide the feverish glitter in his eyes.

"Hello," he introduced himself in a Kentucky drawl. "I'm Mick."

"You'd better come in."

"Thanks," the helmet was dragged off to reveal long auburn hair.

"Come right in." I led the way into the farmhouse and waved towards an easy chair. His heavy boots and dusty apparel didn't bother me. I had long since trusted the Lord with the welfare of my carpet.

"That's right, you're welcome. Make yourself at home. What will it be, coffee?"

"Great, thanks," he looked around, sighing as he shrugged off his jacket and subsided into a chair.

While he drank two cups of coffee in quick succession, I studied his face and thought he looked far from well. I knew that most travelers fear becoming ill on the road where the towns are hundreds of miles apart. He asked if he could stay overnight, saying someone on the road had given him our address. Without preamble I agreed. I directed him to the bathroom then showed him to a bedroom. As I laid another place at the table, I asked God to show me his particular need. At supper Mick did not eat much but drank a lot, then disappeared to his room.

The next morning, the problem was evident. Mick was running an extremely high fever. I bundled him into my car and drove straight to our family doctor in town. An hour later, we were on the way back, only briefly stopping to collect his prescribed medicines from the pharmacy. Mick lay prostrate in the car, already full of antibiotics. We bedded him down in a small spare room in our house next to the bathroom, often used in sickness.

For three days he ran a very high fever. Whenever he managed to stagger to the bathroom, his sweat soaked sheets were changed. Once the fever broke he slept for about two days. But before that, the sound of his vomiting woke me up in the night. Putting on my dressing gown, I went into him. I heard myself say - of all ridiculous things! "Oh Mick, are you sick?" The irrepressible one from Kentucky gave me a speaking look.

"Not, just practicing," he drawled. We laughed about that for a long time.

At one time, when especially pressed for accommodation, I commandeered a garden shed, threw out all the tools and had it scrubbed and whitewashed. After securing any gaps with mosquito gauze, it was furnished with three beds and lockers, including some thick, bright bedspreads of black, red, green and yellow weave. Some fun loving youngsters had a great time fitting up some ultra violet lights so the yellow reflected the fluorescent light and filled the room with purple psychedelic patterns.

Storms were responsible for a number of encounters. A couple of hitchhikers met up in Tanzania. One of them intended to visit Yieldingtree when he reached Lusaka. They joined up and traveled south together, the other coming along to the farm also. They got a lift out from town just as a heavy tropical storm descended and walked in from the main road, arriving extremely bedraggled and tired out. There was no time to learn more than their names in the resulting bustle of offering hot drinks, food, baths and beds.

However, the next morning, while the man who had originally meant to come still slept, the other one walked in to my sitting room asking to talk. I invited him to sit, prepared to help if I could. "I'm a Jew," he said simply, leaning forward in his chair, "and I have been doing a lot of thinking. Can you tell me about Jesus?" This young man found the Savior in recognizing his Messiah. He was one of several Jews that we gladly helped.

Over a hundred miles from the farm, sheltering from a downpour in the early hours of the morning, a group of hippie friends were waiting for the train connection to Lusaka at Kapiri Mposhi, a little town where the railway from East Africa joins the Zambian system. They were returning from India where their spiritual search had not been fulfilled. Now they were nearly out of money, trying hard to reach South Africa to look for work. They were huddled on the porch of a small general store. Hearing their voices and becoming aware of their plight on such a night, the storekeeper invited them to wait inside and offered a hot drink.

In the talk that followed he learned a little of their situation. He and his wife knew us, and before the group left, instructions of how to reach the farm, including the 'phone number, were written down and given to one of the men. He stuffed it in a pocket and forgot about it. Later that day when they could not get on a train out of Lusaka, he remembered and decided to give it a try, thinking it might at least yield some free food and shelter till something else turned up.

Reluctant to admit at first there were six of them, they soon admitted to their true situation and arrangements were made. The farm was fairly full and I already had a whole ham in the oven. Just as well, I thought as I flew round organizing six extra beds. It was a Saturday and the next morning some of the new group accepted our invitation to go with the family to church in town. One of them, enthralled by what he heard, asked if he could go again that night. And that night he found his way to the foot of the cross.

Two of them were a married couple and while the husband went down with pneumonia, his wife also responded to the gospel within a short time. Before the group finally split up another of the men also came to Christ. The two new Christian men spent a lot of time on the farm and ultimately left for Britain, later to train for the ministry.

A young farm worker and his wife disillusioned by poor job prospects, left England to travel. Having reached Zambia they planned to stay with us for a couple of nights. They became interested in our farm and stayed on to lend a hand. Through Gordon, they met a Christian rancher from further up country and from him received a job offer. Not only did the couple both come to Christ, but by taking up the job offer, their prospects improved dramatically and ultimately they came to own their own farm.

Not only did we work together and seek to share our faith with all that came to us, we also took pleasure in sharing God's creation. Africa in all its richness of flora and fauna was endlessly fascinating. Gordon was quite knowledgeable and from time to time would take a group into the bush. Particularly when overseas agricultural students were with us, he would show them Zambia's sugar growing area, the big cattle ranches. Kariba Dam, with its kapenta fishing boats and pleasure craft could be done as a day trip occasionally. It was also possible for him with his many contacts to arrange study and work facilities at such places for the students.

Chapter 12
The Storm from the South

In keeping pace with the years and expansion of our activities, we were always building. Even before Hal joined us as farm manager, we employed a full time builder and Chabaila, our farm carpenter, was kept busy on either the houses, the camp or new farm buildings.

Chabaila was middle-aged when he came to us after his employers left the country. Trained on the Copper mines as a fine woodworker, he worked for several years on our neighbor's ranch and could turn his hand to anything. Whether it was making furniture, setting the roof timbers of a new building or stringing wire for a new paddock fence, everything he did was meticulously right first time. He was a tall, quiet *bambo*. Before coming to us he had lost a finger in a threshing machine accident and his wrinkled face was marred by one eye having been damaged by a spitting cobra. But he had such natural kindliness and dignity, one was hardly aware of this defect.

Early one morning, I asked Chabaila to make me six seed boxes, wanting the job to be done quickly. I expected them in an hour or so. When they had not materialized by midday, I went to his workshop. There I found him carefully finishing the last planed, tongued-and-grooved work of art. It seemed almost shame to put soil in them.

Another large house had evolved beyond the cluster of farm office and store sheds, not far from our gate onto the public road. Standing high above the cattle drift across the river, Bethesda House housed the farm manager, with a tiny guest wing beyond the kitchen and an additional self-contained bed-sit over the garage. It contained a huge circular dining table that Chabaila built in the room. Later we added a siren that could be heard over the entire farm in case of fire or other danger.

One Sunday morning, after the church service, we were introduced to a family who had recently arrived from the north. The couple had three children and was looking for work and housing in Lusaka. We had the bare beginnings of another house on the farm, which had for the moment, come to a standstill. Since this gentleman was a builder, Gordon offered accommodation in exchange for his skills. When the building was complete and named "Sharon Cottage" the family lived there for a period. The wife, Pam, helped us in the house and library, and her husband found work in the town. "Sharon Cottage" was situated beyond our house. The cottage stood

94

behind the cassia trees that flanked the area set aside for the overland trucks. It was a bungalow with three bedrooms, kitchen, bathroom, dining room and a good sitting room. A stone chimney and fireplace was added later, built by another skilled traveler, his contribution for staying with us.

As the buildings grew, so the crops expanded. We sold off produce by the half -ton daily load after taking all we needed. My husband's particular pleasure was the flower garden that swept in smooth terraces down to the river under the wide shade of jacaranda and flame trees. To one side the rose garden led to a small rise overlooking the pond where a Japanese plum tree and a lime's dark leaves stood out against the mauve cloud of the pungent ginger blossom. Across the lawn, a clump of tall bamboo clung to the riverbank, above which the rising land was covered with a blue gum, eucalyptus plantation painstakingly planted by us in the early years.

The vegetable garden attracted me more than flowers, perhaps because of its connection with being able to feed the children. As I took pleasure in the feel of a warm brown egg in the palm of my hand, so the rain-shiny skin of an eggplant, or the crisp snap as the green peppers were picked and the cool symmetry of glossy cucumbers, never failed to please me. My earliest attempts at getting the sequence planting right so we had a continuous supply, together with an even more premature effort with the language produced my first racial crisis.

At this time we only had a couple of workers to help with the stock and, needing help in the carrot bed, I attempted to explain what I wanted.

"Bwerani, bwerani kuno," I called across to the nearest man. "Come, come here!"

"Tengani khasu ku khya," I instructed as he hurried up. Well, I thought, at least he understood that, as he went off to the shed and came back with a hoe. Then came the dangerous bit as I tried to explain I wanted the weeds hoed out and the carrots thinned. He kept nodding so I went back to the house. Just before tea he appeared at the back door indicating he had finished. I followed him to the garden.

The newly turned earth now flanked the rampant weeds while all the carrots lay in wilting heaps along the paths. I very nearly screamed at the man, but I managed to control my frustration. I suddenly saw the funny side of it all and weakly leant against a fence post as gales of laughter overcame me. The man studied me with a pained expression but I was unable to explain. I merely waved him away and mopped my face thinking, "I'll try tomorrow. Wow, I do believe I can take Africa on the chin and laugh." But it would not always be so.

A dark element had entered our lives and its tentacles reached out and touched us all. In the midst of peace and openness, of spiritual harvest and rejoicing, terrible things were happening in the name of national freedom and their counterpart surfaced in personal attitudes and other odd incidents. Scattered here and there as the months went by, it was hard at first to see the threat for what it was. But it was to rise and devour us all.

An unknown group from another province, booked to use our facility across the river. There was nothing on their letter-headed inquiry to suggest they were anything other than a genuine Christian group, although we had not before come across them. They only wanted five days, so in good faith they were booked in and duly arrived. Gordon, who had been away at the onset, came back and seemed very unhappy about it. But they had only three more days, so we decided to allow them to finish. However, our staff, whose living quarters were nearby were uneasy, and there was talk of political, not gospel, meetings and strange rituals instead of evening campfire singsongs. In anger, Gordon said he would go over after our evening meal and see for himself. Taking a good torch, he went off about 7:30pm.

Time passed and the children went to bed. I took hot drinks into the group round the log fire in the sitting room. Time sped by in familiar fashion in lively discussion. When everyone had retired for the night, I became aware of the late hour. Now I was getting worried and unaccountably I remembered Gordon telling me that during his time in government service in Nyasaland, he had gone to see an African tribal initiation ceremony, forbidden to whites. Surely this could not be something equally illicit? Pictures of political unrest whipped up by tribal fervor giving rise to troubles in the 60's in Nyasaland and N. Rhodesia pre-independence struggles, gnawed at the edges of my mind.

When Gordon came back he was gray-faced and uncommunicative. He pushed my questions aside and tersely told me to go to bed. As I lay awake, I could hear him gasping and gagging in the bathroom. I never did learn just what he had seen as, he admitted later, he watched hidden behind a tree. By the next morning the people had cleared off. The incident slipped behind us as more pressing concerns had our attention.

Among our staff at this time we had two brothers who worked in the dairy and garden. One Saturday, after drinking rather a lot of homemade *chibuku* beer they had fallen into a fierce argument and a fight broke out. Naturally things that happened in off-duty hours were none of our concern, and we knew nothing until one of them, our off-duty dairyman, arrived at the kitchen door at dawn on Sunday. He was badly hung over, with a hideous wounded face where part of his nose had been bitten clean off. He pathetically offered me the shriveled piece in a brown paper bag, still covered with blood and sand. Would I take him to the hospital? His brother reported to work on Monday morning with half his cheek torn away. It was far too late to restore the nose, and the other man's cheek puckered as the crater healed. Though they continued to work for us and we had no specific knowledge of what had so disturbed their usual good relationship, nonetheless they were no longer good friends as before. Seeing their mutilated faces around the place was a disturbing reminder of the latent savagery around us.

The "winds of change" referred to by the British Parliamentary leader, Harold Macmillan way back in 1960, were beginning to be seriously felt. It had been acknowledged long since in the South African Parliament that the African National Congress was awakening everywhere. The wind of change was blowing through the whole continent and the growth of this consciousness was already a political fact. The "lion of revolution" had stirred and was beginning to roar. Forces were set in motion that could not be quelled. A more complex future faced everyone.

Late in the 1970's the unrest in S. Rhodesia was gathering momentum. It was no longer safe to travel through that country and the overland expedition companies, who were booked well ahead had to adapt a policy of driving south to Lusaka, flying their passengers over, who were then met in South Africa to complete the trip. Those joining expeditions in Johannesburg to travel north were flown to Lusaka in like manner. If the southbound truck was not available to meet them, we collected and accommodated them. At this period it was not desirable to pitch tents that could be mistaken for military from the air, so the passengers came into the guestrooms.

It also meant that temporary workshop facilities were set up on the farm to service these trucks and again there were many opportunities to assist or aid the drivers. If a driver became ill or had an accident, we were there to help if we could. Friendships were formed and in due course a spiritual harvest was reaped.

In 1977, the ripples of conflict in S. Rhodesia were spreading further and further. Military roadblocks and guards on all bridges were a constant burr under the residents and visitors alike. Most of the travelers who came reported problems.

By early 1978, the difficulties of traveling around that part of Africa became more pronounced and the trekking all but ceased. The unrest was being communicated to residents in Zambia and we could not but be affected by the struggle across her borders. Shortages of foodstuffs were becoming more common and people became wary of strangers.

In the over spill of the civil war that was escalating in Southern Rhodesia, Zambia was also suffering, playing host to thousands of freedom fighters behind her borders who inhabited large camps in many areas. Throughout 1978 conditions deteriorated rapidly and tension gripped the nation. Several of the camps had been bombed and everywhere the pressure on ordinary people were intense. There were increasing numbers of hostile incidents and suspicion and fear ruled.

On the farm, those of us in leadership positions often met together for prayer. On one particular afternoon, Hal stopped work and with Rose, who had been laboring in intercessory prayer, Gordon, Pam and I joined Hal and Jo at their request. When we learned of the massacre of the Elim missionaries, only a few weeks earlier, the news sent a tremor through us all. For although the incident had been in eastern Southern Rhodesia, a long way off, we were very aware that the whole territory was poised for the mayhem to spread. Jo was extremely frightened but hid it well.

We sat around taking turns to pray. Clearly Rose's spirit was heavily burdened. She had always displayed great insight into problems and now she voiced again her disquiet. Previously, she had hinted to me about 'problems' she saw among us without being specific and I had responded on this occasion, by asking her to go on praying for us all and thanking her for her support.

Later, the Holy Spirit chided me for ducking the responsibility of pinning her down at the time. Now she became more vocal in the Spirit and uttered a grave warning. Speaking of a great darkness that would come over us, she called on each one of us to seek God's face as we faced this dire threat. She concluded by saying that those who kept our eyes fixed on the Lord through the storm that was coming would rejoice in the light to come afterwards.

Afterwards, I pondered much on her strange choice of words. Talking it over with Jo and Hal later, I realized their fears were very real, while I, thinking only vaguely about the gathering problems to the south, was more interested in the "light that was to come." Pam had made no contribution at all while Gordon was very quiet during the prayers and even afterwards at home, made no comment.

Weeks passed and Pam and her husband were due some leave and they went to England. Next Rose returned to Australia. Gordon announced his intention of going overseas to take our daughter on a trip to Europe in her college vacation. He was gone by the end of July.

The increased tension in the country led to military roadblocks, and we heard reports of more atrocities below the border. We had a camp of several thousand S. Rhodesian Freedom fighters only 4 km up the road. The district began to be plagued by small incidents, the farm workers were worried about their women and sent them all back to their villages in the deep bush. The

Christians among the staff met with me daily for prayer as a new menace threatened from the skies.

Up to this point, our local farm workers had only looked up in wonder and excitement if a low flying airplane came over. Now the cry went up "Ndeke" Ndeke!" And as the low flying planes of the Rhodesian Air Force screamed in at speeds that gave us practically no warning, buckets and hoes would go flying as our workers would fling themselves in the nearest ditch, while I, a child of World War II, hit the floor in the house. Empty 30mm cannon shells bounced on the lawn as the planes commenced their run up to the freedom fighters' camp. The noise was deafening.

On the next-door property, two men were killed one day. Plumes of smoke could be seen above the trees. A property, only a short distance from ours, had been purchased by the freedom fighters. They used it to conceal a fuel dump. This bombing caused a major conflagration.

At night we sometimes heard the muffled explosions as bombs went off when the Rhodesian forces raided the city, trying to root out rebels hiding there.

We heard tales of one commando raid that brought helicopters down in a residential area just as folk were leaving their driveways to take their children to school. And still Gordon did not return but wrote instead that he would stay on and return in time for Christmas, traveling with Grace who would be finishing her college course then. Meanwhile the family who had formerly lived in Sharon Cottage returned. Air raids became more frequent and caused widespread disruption.

In the midst of all this, Ken arrived. Hearing the dogs barking, I put down my rolling pin and opened the back door to find a dejected figure below the step. His bony knees showed through torn jeans, he wore broken shoes and no socks. Tired eyes looked up from a dusty face. His thin shoulders supported a tattered backpack that appeared to be almost empty.

"Mrs. Bland?"

"Yes, hello. Come in." I held the door wide and invited him to enter. He let his pack fall by the door and slowly walked into my kitchen.

"Would you like a cup of coffee?" He nodded silently and slid onto the stool I pulled forward. I pushed a mug of coffee and the sugar toward him and watched his gaunt face as he picked up the mug with both grubby hands and gulped quickly. Silently, he accepted a refill. Still silent, I turned to the fridge and quickly assembled a sandwich. I put it down in front of him and went back to making my pie for lunch.

"Thanks." He tried a tremulous smile as he answered in an Australian accent.

After a bath, another good meal and the loan of a razor, Ken fell asleep in the cabin where he slept the clock round. Over the next few days he told me of his extraordinary trek. As a hitchhiker, he decided to remain in S. Rhodesia before the escalation of the civil war and found a job. He married a Rhodesian policewoman. Later, a foolish error got him thrown out of the country. Unable to get back, or find a job in South Africa, he hitch hiked through Botswana and entered Zambia that way. He had been given our name and address. So now, extremely anxious about his wife who was pregnant, he used up his dwindling resources to reach Lusaka.

In Lusaka he was picked up on the street by the police, thrown into jail as a political suspect, only to find he had lost the paper bearing our name and address. Two days later he was released and told to quit Zambia immediately. He found a lift to the Malawi border, some four hundred miles to the east. In Malawi, he wandered around sleeping rough, selling off his few possessions in order to eat. Some time later, he stumbled across some people who knew us and gave him our name as being the folk most likely to help him.

So Ken decided to return and hitched all the way back. In Lusaka he collapsed in the street and was helped by someone who drove him to our gate. Up to that point he had not heard from his wife and she, in the meantime, had suffered a miscarriage. But he was driven by his determination not to leave Africa without her.

Chapter 13
The Raid

An air of palpable tension gripped the nation. Rumors abounded. Tales of commando like raids, upon pockets of freedom fighters taking refuge in the city, were given credence by sounds of explosions and gunfire. Some nights we could hear bombs going off. Travel after dark was fraught with danger. In the daytime, we would often be confronted with the sudden appearance of soldiers and turned aside without explanation. Military roadblocks were everywhere and we had to endure at least one every time we left the farm drive. Often ordered out of one's vehicle while it was searched, even to the point of having the seats removed. It was tedious and nerve-wracking. And it was not even our war.

Now the air raids by the Rhodesian air force, aimed at the freedom fighter camps, were almost daily. We became used to seeing long convoys of assorted vehicles wending their way into the city. Crowded with the wounded, they made their way to the hospital that was now under military control. On Tuesday November 7th Lusaka's main street erupted into violence and the police were rounding up unfamiliar Europeans without ceremony.

Over recent years when a property had changed hands, it had become harder than ever to be certain who one's new neighbors really were. In several instances, freedom fighters moved in without their true identities or intentions being evident. A neighboring farmer was killed while walking on his land with his wife and child. Because of the number of freedom fighters in the area it had become unwise to venture over the river. On the hill across the river, on our boundary anti-air craft guns had been placed. The Rhodesian civil war was being partly fought over our heads, owing to the large numbers of Nkomo's Matebele freedom fighters in Zambia. The other faction fought behind the Mozambique border under Mugabe the Shona leader.

The flow of visitors virtually came to a stop. It was not wise to travel and cross-country trekking had ceased. However there were quite a lot of people living on the farm.

Hal and Jo were at Bethesda, the farm manager's house, with our young Swedish secretary living in the little flat over the garage. At the main house with me were our two sons, and two American boys, who were the sons of missionary friends living almost two hundred miles away. They were boarding with us to go to school with our boys. And there was Ken, the

Australian. Pam and her family were back at Sharon Cottage.

That Tuesday evening, everyone gathered at the main house for supper and prayer. Jo was the only exception because she had fallen and broken her leg only a day or two before so she was resting. We shared Psalm 91.

On Wednesday morning November 8th I took Stuart and the American boys to school in Jo's car, as my car was giving a little trouble and Ken said he would take a look at it. Since breaking her leg, Jo was confined to her bed as her entire leg was in plaster. Hal had loaded up the pickup truck early and gone to town on farm business. Pam had gone up to give Jo some personal assistance while I took the children. Planning to do some shopping, I said I would stay in town that morning and not return until it was time to bring the American children home at lunchtime.

It was not long after I had left for town that morning that a large group of freedom fighters, heavily armed with AK47 rifles, moved on to our farm. They roughed up several farm workers and caught Hal on his return as he parked the pickup truck near the farm office. They manhandled him into one of their vehicles and took off. The ladies knew nothing. At the first sign of trouble, Jo's house servant disappeared without saying a word.

Shortly afterwards while returning from Jo's house, Pam was caught in the lane and bundled into another vehicle which also left the farm. Ken, busy working on my car near the main house, was also captured and taken off, in my car.

Sonja, our secretary was in the study talking to our youngest son, who had stayed home that day because of a slight indisposition. Suddenly they realized a large group of heavily armed men had surrounded the house and gained entry. The men forced the two young people out at bayonet point. Told to get all the keys, they were then pushed round all the rooms and outbuildings. Any doors for which they could not produce a key were bashed open. The children's dog went berserk but fearing it would get shot, they managed to bring it under control. Sonja was very slightly built and though in her early twenties looked a teenager. She was dressed in jeans and a little check shirt. Perhaps the men took them for two kids and therefore did not harm her. It was very frightening but both young people kept their heads.

When the group reached Jo's house it was the first inkling that she had of something being very wrong. Apart from wondering where her house servant had got to, Jo has been unperturbed as she was used to Hal being busy out on the farm for long periods of time. The freedom fighter prodded the youngsters forwards into her bedroom then stopped short and said, "Oh Madam, you are sick." He then inexplicably backed out leaving the bewildered trio. They heard men shouting to each other about coming back, the sound of vehicles driving away, then there was silence.

They were all quite badly shaken, but Jo was mature and spiritually strong. She held them together and prayed, bearing in mind that I was due back soon.

About 1:o'clock I drove in and having a message for Hal went to his house first. I left the two American boys in the car where they had fallen asleep, and ran up the steps to the front porch expecting to find Hal and Jo at lunch. Instead my son ran to meet me looking very upset. When he explained what had happened I went into Jo to see what we could do. The four of us hastily conferred, agreeing that it would be difficult to evacuate her and the others in her small car. We decided I should go for help.

I dashed to the car to find the boys awake. Telling them to lie down on the floor of the car and to stay there, I warned them not to be frightened, but said there were robbers about and if they jumped out at us from the bush I was not going to stop. Brave words - but my heart was already thumping with alarm and I was frightened.

Spinning the little car round and putting my foot down, I wondered if we would make it out to the main road safely. Were these men waiting in the bush? Why had it happened? Who were they after? With a huge sigh of relief I got out onto the main road without incident and sped towards town. About a mile down the road was the headquarters of a Safari company who knew us. They bought fresh produce from our farm to fly to their hunting camps. I turned in their gate with the notion of asking for their help. But none was available. With adrenaline pumping, I careered out of there and headed for town.

What to do? In what order should I do it? Very much aware that the two boys were frightened, I strove for control and talked to the boys quietly. It was very hot and perspiration was pouring off me. I strove to control my jumping nerves and prayed. I asked God to help me, to clear my mind so I could think of the best way of dealing with this crisis. Although my heart was thumping at an alarming rate, immediately my mind became calm. A clear idea of what to do came to me. I told the boys where we were going and drove through town, taking the Great East Road out to our pastor at the manse.

After the initial shock of my arrival in the middle of their lunch, the pastor and his wife took the boys. I made arrangements to contact their parents over the Africa Evangelical Mission radio. Figuring what to do about the others left out on the farm was more difficult. My suggestion that somebody in the church might be found, with a suitable vehicle, to go out to the farm to rescue the three seemed best and I had to leave the pastor to do what he could do. In this he was successful and the church was alerted to pray.

After that, I went to the Police to report the incident, thinking naively it would not take long, but in that I was very much mistaken. I reported at the front desk and was immediately hustled upstairs into a large room. Several high-ranking officers questioned me at length. Other officers and paramilitary were summoned and after that it became somewhat of an ordeal. I did not know then, that our incident was not the only one that day, though the only one involving kidnapping. An hour later they let me out but my relief was short lived. I was pushed into another room with a policewoman guard and told to wait.

Dead silence reigned, broken only by the frantic buzzing of a trapped fly on the dusty window ledge. The African policewoman sat stoically looking down at her hands outstretched on the desk. I sat on the only other chair watching the clock on the wall. Dying for a drink and desperate to go, I sat, in a disheveled post shock reaction. I tried not to think about what might be happening at the farm, and wished the hands of the clock would move.

I tried to talk to the policewoman, to ask her if she knew what was happening now. But she only shuffled her feet and stabbing a forefinger in my direction, she said, "You don't talk, you stay." Desperate to escape, to reach my embassy, I fixed my attention on my clenched hands in my lap and silently prayed. After a long forty- five minutes an officer came to the door and said I could go.

About that time, some brave young African men from our church were on their way to the farm in a borrowed estate wagon. They carried Jo out and laid her on a mattress on the vehicle floor, and with Sonja, they drove to town safely. They took Jo to a friend's house and Sonja to the manse. Meanwhile our son had managed to find the spare keys to the farm pickup truck left outside the office, and drove it off the farm behind them. Later we learnt that the freedom fighters did return before dark that same night and took possession.

I left the police station and went straight to the British Embassy to report. The supportive diplomatic machinery was set in motion, the embassy acting on behalf of Ken also since the nearest Australian consul was in Dar-es-Salaam, Tanzania. They also undertook to contact Gordon in England.

It was after 5:30pm before I reached the school to collect Stuart who was worried because I was so late. At the Manse I was relieved to find everyone safe and Jo had been delivered into good hands. A group of supportive church members arrived. Pam's children were with her husband who was making his own arrangements. The radio message brought the parents of the

American boys, and Sonja's father from Mpongwe, to swiftly to take them home.

It was all too soon to know what we were really up against. I accepted accommodation for the boys at one house while I arranged to stay with a friend, a doctor, conscious that I might need her professionally as I faced the total responsibility in this horrific situation.

It was very late before I got to bed exhausted. The clothes I wore were all I had, so I laundered them in the bathroom knowing they would be dry by morning. My last waking thoughts were a prayer for all those so cruelly snatched away.

Unknown to me that night, heroic efforts were being made by a Christian in Lusaka who both knew our family and by accident almost, had a contact with a very high-ranking freedom fighter. Making the most of his opportunity, he pleaded on our behalf and risked putting himself in danger, but God was with him. Before daylight, two Zambia police cars were dispatched to the area beyond our farm, and the missing trio was 'found.' All the details of that night were shrouded in secrecy in the highly sensitive political circumstances. But it was enough for me to know God had answered prayer and be thankful.

In the grace of God, Pam was put in one police car while Hal and Ken traveled in the other. Her face bore a mass of contusions, two ribs were broken and she had been raped. Exhausted, she vomited all over the car and policemen asked her where they should take her. Delivered to the manse, she was safe. But for the men it was very different.

A message from Lusaka Police reached me just after 6:00am. Hal and Ken were detained at the central police station. I hurried there immediately. I had to plead repeatedly and insistently before I was allowed to see them. Shocked to find them dumped on the cell floor, watched over by indifferent guards, it took a while for the truth to sink in. Our men were being treated as suspects.

No aid or even a drink had been given them. Both were filthy, covered in sand and blood, and in shock. Ken was barefoot, his feet slashed to ribbons. He had been strung up in a tree with wire and suffered a blow across the throat with a rifle butt, so he could not speak and could barely swallow. Hal was badly knocked about and was bleeding in several places. I found out later that while he was being tortured, a soldier had taunted Ken with threats, while he brandished a snapshot of Siboniso, his native Rhodesian wife, which he had taken from Ken's room. This was seen as a piece of damming evidence that he was involved in the southern conflict, and that was part of their motive for this outrage.

Horrified, I pleaded for aid for them but was told, we would have to wait till the day shift came at 8:0am. Telling Hal and Ken I would get back as soon as I could, I drove back to where I was staying and put washcloths, a towel and a bottle of water in a basket with some antiseptic and a Thermos of hot sweet coffee. Armed with this, I dashed back to the police station and demanded to be let in again. I did what little I could and stayed with them. Maybe when the day staff came on duty, we could sort this out, but it was a forlorn hope.

On the way back to the police station, I diverted to collect Stuart from his lodging. I felt I needed someone with me and it was a very fortunate decision. When the day shift came on, all my pleas fell on deaf ears and I realized it was not going to be that easy. Not until I found myself once again shut in an upstairs office, did I begin to comprehend the deep atmosphere of suspicion surrounding our men. The police would not allow them to be released. Even my pleas that they be given some medical aid fell on deaf ears.

Nearly two hours went by. I became more and more anxious about Hal and Ken's state, and worried about Stuart waiting downstairs. This time there was several police and paramilitary personnel in the room, yet a man in plain clothes was in charge. All my efforts to keep a semblance of control in the situation proved useless. I became more frightened by the minute, doing my best to answer the barrage of questions from the men. I did not understand their attitude and felt threatened.

The door opened behind me and to my surprise and relief, the Director of the Churches Medical Association in Zambia, walked in. He had stopped at the police station on an errand and seen Stuart hovering anxiously near the front desk. Because he knew the family and heard about the incident, he spoke to Stuart who poured out his anxiety for me, only too glad to see a friendly face. He offered to help.

He came into the room where I was seated at a table with my back to the door, surrounded by interrogators. He stood beside me and placed a hand on my shoulder with a slight pressure, as if to say 'leave this to me'. He had a quiet but very commanding presence and as soon as he got involved things began to move.

It was agreed that the two men could be taken to hospital provided they were under armed guards and we used our own transport. It took some time for a policeman to be detailed to accompany us, and for him to then draw a weapon. Finally we were able to go down to the cells and get Hal and Ken into the Director's car it being larger than mine. Once on the way to the hospital I felt better, but the situation was still difficult. At the hospital casualty department the Staff was uncertain whether to admit the men, and Ken panicked. But in the grace of God, the first nurse to reach his stretcher

106

was a Christian, someone he had already met at the farm. Finally they were admitted - with the armed policeman on guard beside their beds.

Next I needed a permit to visit, since the hospital was full of injured Rhodesian freedom fighters at that time and under military control. This proved difficult. Since I was not actually a relative of either of the men, the authorities were adamant. I just caught the Director who was on the point of leaving to resume his business. Could he help? Once again he spoke on my behalf and since he carried considerable clout, won me a permit to visit at any time. It was doubly important because I was the only liaison between all victims, the police and the Embassy.

Now this became my daily round. The Australian consul in Dar-es-Salaam arranged for me to speak on the telephone directly to Canberra to plead for assistance for Ken, and especially for permission to get his wife out of Rhodesia and into Australia. The Vice Consul subsequently traveled to Lusaka to expedite Ken's release and travel to Australia.

At the hospital, the whole incident together with the care and interest that Hal and Ken received, especially from members of the Nurses Christian Fellowship, generated a significant interest among the other staff. In the two weeks immediately afterwards, almost fifty Gideon New Testaments were distributed upon individual request.

Throughout the emergency I had a very strong inner peace. Despite the nerve racking circumstances that took a heavy toll on emotions and energy, the deep sense of having God near me, almost tangible at times, never left. The words of Isaiah in Chapter 26 v 3 came to mind several times: *"You will keep in perfect peace him whose mind is steadfast, because he trusts in you."* Indeed, the deep down sense of peace was very real.

Chapter 14
Echoes of Conflict

Although my inner peace sustained my spirit, the daily pressures were all too real. By the weekend I was too exhausted to get to church and had to rest before and after completing my round of hospital and police. The police had instructed me to report every day while the emergency lasted and it all took time. For this reason I was not there to hear Pam's testimony in the church that Sunday, nor was I able to be present at her interview with the British Broadcasting Corporation reporter in Lusaka that week.

A couple of days later, I went over the manse to see Pam. While I was talking to her in the bedroom, the phone rang in the hall and she was called. To my astonishment I heard her mention my husband's name so I ran out to ask to speak to him and had to be quite insistent before she relinquished the phone to me. He made only a brief, somewhat perfunctory inquiry after my well being and did not even ask after the boys. Surprisingly, he told me he was taking the time to travel across England to visit the families of Hal and Pam before returning to Lusaka. I felt bewildered, disappointed and very let down, for I had been assured the news of our predicament had reached him without delay. But I also had so much on my mind and comforted myself that he had said he would return in a few days. Only afterwards did I question how he had known Pam's whereabouts. And why had he not attempted to contact me first?

Meanwhile, the pressure of our situation pushed these thoughts aside as I concentrated on the job in hand. A message reached me, brought to town by one of our workers that the Freedom Fighters had left the farm, albeit they were camped only just up the road, and the farm was out of stock feed. I had to plead with the Milling Company to send out ten tons immediately and they were very reluctant. Finally I persuaded them to deliver to a point a mile short of the farm and sent a message back for all the workers to go out to that place and prepare to pack the load in. The truck duly found the workers at the designated spot and after the first tractor-trailer load was on its way, the rest was unloaded at the side of the road where it was guarded until the job was done. Meanwhile, I'd had a real hard job to persuade the bank to release the money for this load that had to be paid for up front as was the custom. But God was with me that day and even in this I prevailed.

In between hospital visits, reporting daily to the police and embassy, as requested, I was kept busy with the needs of my sons and Ken. I had to shop for things we all needed and spend time talking to our Bank Manager, trying to anticipate the farm needs though I little firm information. Ken had an operation to repair the damage to his feet and all the while both men were still being watched by an armed guard beside their beds. For days I had been wearing the same clothes, washing them every night and ironing them first thing every morning. Now some gifts of clothing arrived for us and I could temporarily outfit myself and find something for my boys. Our bank was so wary I was trying not to spend on anything other than absolute essentials

But the next day when I called in to report to the police as requested, the atmosphere had abruptly changed. Suddenly my reception felt hostile again. I was more closely questioned, separated apart with guards and hurried down the steps of the police station, with two silent policewomen holding me on either side. No one would answer questions and tell me where we were going. In desperation I saw an acquaintance approach and called out to him to inform the Embassy if I did not report in three hours. The policemen bundled me into an unmarked car. Both the driver and his companion were in plain clothes, neither would answer any question. Even if I had a better command of the local language, I would have gained no clue. They were silent. We left town and took the road west and not until the car turned into the farm drive did I admit how frightened I had been that I might have been taken somewhere more sinister.

I was not prepared for what met me at the farm. The workers were lined up on one side of the lawn, armed police and paramilitary stood on every side. Spent ammunition lay scattered about with a lot of other rubbish. My two particular guards stayed very close, even going with me to the bathroom, searching my bag. A heavily armed man with an inscrutable manner took charge. I took him to be a paramilitary officer. He questioned me at length over a table where a couple of hand guns, aerials maps of the farm, Hal's radio - which used to save him endless walking all over the property - all lay in a welter of loose ammunition and farm papers. Even the old binoculars, which we used for bird watching looked anything but innocent in the midst of all this.

Suggestions that all this stuff was connected with ground- to-air communications and my denial did not seem to register, as did my denial of any connection with the weapons. I could only repeat, no one on the farm kept a gun, finding it quite impossible to guess if I was believed or not. After a while, I was taken on a tour of the whole place again, and the devastation wrought by the attackers sent shock waves through me.

The main house was a mess, broken ornaments and rubbish in the sitting room. All small loose items had vanished, linen, tape players, radios and kitchen equipment. Mirrors and clocks had been ripped off walls, some curtains hung drunkenly on broken rails and some of them were ripped and thrown across the garden. One mattress, stripped of bedding was halfway through window, in another room one whole bed was gone, the twin bed-frame upended against the wall. The safe door swung on one bent hinge, empty. One of the family passports, was found in a flowerbed, ripped up, one was found in the neighboring bush days later, other important papers were never found.

Everywhere, drawers were pulled out and scattered, some missing altogether. The pantry, fridge and freezers were stripped and bleach had been thrown on bathroom, hall and kitchen floor taking out the color, leaving ugly pale blotches. In our office-cum study, papers and files from the filing cabinets were dumped on the floor, empty boxes of family photos were scattered everywhere, the whole mess covered in flour and then the squeezed contents of several tubes of duplicating ink. Evidently the soldiers had walked through this, for there were imprints of heavy boots over the papers and in the hallway.

The guards still close about me, we then toured the rest of the building. Where no key was available, the doors were smashed open. One heavy steel door bore the imprint of a particularly ferocious attack in the pitted surface around the broken lock. In the guestrooms, which had, at this time, been unoccupied, similar destruction was found. Ken's room had been savagely ripped apart, but Sharon Cottage and Bethesda House were hardly touched. So it seemed the farm itself was the main target.

I had not been allowed to talk to any of the farm workers and was unsure what was happening to them. With none of my questions answered, I could but guess what the outcome would be. Then I was taken back to the car and returned to town.

Once back at the police station to my relieved surprise, I was released in the car park. I drove to the Embassy, still feeling shaken. It was a comfort to find that they had been told of my unceremonious exit, and to be assured that inquiries would have been made, had I not returned that afternoon.

Meanwhile Hal and Jo, who were still with her friend, began preparations to return to England. I was offered the use of a house that belonged to friends who were away on leave.

During the following week I had many opportunities to thank God for our workers' faithfulness, though many of the stories were only told some time afterwards. After the initial confrontation with the attackers, the workers had fled shutting themselves in their houses. One or two intrepid souls crept forth the next day and very cautiously came to see if they could reach the stock unmolested. They were not harmed and so water was pumped, the stock cared for and gradually the most important jobs were done.

Thereafter our African workers bravely came to work every day, pumped water and looked after the stock. They were allowed to move about fairly freely and in the course of the next few days, as the danger subsided a little, they achieved some remarkable things. One of them found the keys to Stuart's abandoned motorbike and surreptitiously walked it through the bush to town where it was eventually returned to him. This relieved pressure on transport. Stuart, who was in his senior year, could now take his brother with him to school on the pillion.

Our dog was found and brought into town to us by a farm worker. Other workers took empty stock feed bags and stealthily packed all the books from the library, back packed them across the river and hid them in their own houses. Someone else reached my bedroom, grabbed a bag and stuffed it with a few remaining odds and ends. That too found its way to me in town.

When Gordon returned, nearly a week later, he left Grace in England. He appeared irritable with the inevitable untidiness in our quarters, which I thought was unreasonable. Surely he could understand how difficult it was trying to find a place to put piles of donated clothes and the flotsam of rescued bits and pieces. True, things overflowed onto the floor but I was ragged with tiredness and strain. He was impatient with my attempts to share some of the wonderful things I felt sure God had done, and was indeed still doing, in the crisis. He cut me off with "you've handled it all wrong. Now leave everything to me." Within the hour, he was off to see Pam.

The only thing that he brought me from England was a satin nightdress. Not only had he not attempted to find out what I needed, I discovered later he had brought an identical one for Pam.

After his return, he was advised by the authorities not to attempt to try and get back on the farm to live until they advised him it was safe. However, he had taken to going out for a short while each day in an effort to get things together and keep the farm going. The invaders had killed and made off with some livestock and raided the garden. Also following his long absence and Hal having left the scene, he had a lot to sort out, customers to contact and so on.

One day in my absence from the house, Gordon sent the farm tractor and trailer with an assortment of stuff from the farm, odd clothes, kitchen odds and ends, papers, office stuff and books. This hotchpotch of miscellaneous grubby, broken and torn things had been stuffed into several old 44 - gallon oil drums. They had no trace of oil left in them, having stood out on the farm as water barrels and storage containers for years. But they were old, dirty and rusty. The men brought them straight into the house and left them on our friend's sitting room carpet. Why our benefactor's house servant had not said to leave them outside where there was an adequate covered veranda, I will never know.

Before I arrived, the father of our benefactor's wife had called in to see how we were getting on. Upon seeing this mess, he was very upset. He was a dear elderly saint whom we knew well, but when I got there he was very distressed. Moreover he was extremely angry. In vain I tried to tell him it was none of my doing. My distress over this incident was a catalyst. Suddenly all the latent fear, the exhaustion, the uncertainty hit me like an avalanche, leaving me sick and shaking unable to do another thing.

The next day when a Zambian police car drew up, I was alone in the house, and was so nervous I had made sure both back and front doors were locked. I watched the policemen approach but would not open the door. Instead I backed up the hall and they repeatedly pounded on the door, I backed further and further through the house till I was in a bedroom pressed against the wall. Mercifully they gave up and drove off but I was left shaking and very aware of how vulnerable and shattered I had become. When Gordon came he went back to talk to the police who asked him to return with me.

The police had been making exhaustive inquiries but thankfully there were plenty of people around to vouch for us, to corroborate my story.

Therefore when we arrived at the police station the atmosphere was almost cordial. The group that had formerly interrogated me now shook me by the hand, explaining that the result of their inquiries had completely exonerated me. They hoped I would not be discouraged from continuing my "Christian Social Service."

However, we had been advised it was unwise to attempt to return to the farm. The unrest in the area was continuing and until things were stabilized, we should stay away. Gordon bought air tickets the next day, and in a couple of days, sent the boys and I to England. My first task was to get the boys newly outfitted but before I had time to concentrate on myself, Siboniso arrived.

When I went to say goodbye to Ken who was still in hospital, he was much recovered and rejoicing in a wonderful answer to prayer. When an Australian newspaper picked up the story of the raid on our farm, Ken's father read of it and managed to get a phone call to Ken's bedside in Lusaka's hospital. He had left the family when Ken was a small boy and this was the first direct contact Ken received. They had wept and been reconciled over the phone.

Now Ken was anxious about his wife. Getting Siboniso out of Salisbury, S. Rhodesia in such a time of danger was a miracle of God's love and provision. The Australian Vice Consul had come down to Lusaka from Dar-es-Salaam to personally look into Ken's situation, and put into motion arrangements for his repatriation. But S. Rhodesia, since U.D.I. and seven years of civil war, was a very difficult place indeed, especially in Siboniso's circumstances.

A message was sent, via missionaries in Malawi, to a contact in Salisbury to inform Siboniso of the plan to get her out. She had no passport. A Christian pastor assisted her in getting a travel document and drove her over the border to the home of an Afrikaans pastor in Pretoria. Meanwhile, in London I was able to arrange her air ticket from Pretoria to Johannesburg, on to London and then to Melbourne, Australia. I had to plead with the UK Immigration Authorities to allow her to fly via London and apply to Heathrow Port Authority for permission for her to land. Wonderfully the Lord made a way and all this was accomplished in a week. I was even able to pay for the ticket in London that she collected at Pretoria airport.

I met Siboniso for the first and last time at London Heathrow where she was formerly released into my custody. She had several hours to wait for her onward flight, so we got a room in the nearest airport hotel where we rested and talked. It was evident this whole series of events had made a deep impression on her. I could only pray it would not end there. From gifts I had received "to meet any needs at the time" I was able to give her a jacket for she had no coat, and a little Australian currency, together with a Bible. She expected to be met by Ken's family and would actually arrive in Melbourne a few days ahead of him. I waved her off the next morning and returned to my mother's house.

The children and I were separate for Christmas. It was lovely to see Grace, but there was not room for us all at Solihull so I sent them all off to their young cousins to have as normal a Christmas as possible while I remained in my brother's house and succumbed with a bad chill.

Stuart flew back in January 1979 to stay in town with friends so he could finish school as he only had a little time left. Bearing in mind his experience in the raid, we decided Jon should remain for the time being. He was to live in his uncle's household and complete his schooling. And as things worked out, he remained thereafter.

While all this was going on, news of our situation had reached many of our extended spiritual family overseas. Over Christmas and New Year many gifts of money had been sent to me. Among them, one specifically designated to replace our kitchen equipment. These gifts were so encouraging because of the expression of love and they helped me believe that we would soon have a restored home someday. I made the most of the money at the January sales, then wondered how to get it out to Zambia. Then the representative of a medical mission supply organization contacted me and offered assistance. This was of the utmost help and very deeply appreciated.

In Zambia, it was two weeks before Gordon could return to live on the farm. Though things were still unsettled, he felt our living was in jeopardy and therefore he should be on the farm. Accordingly he returned just before Christmas and wrote to tell me. He was feeling the loss of Hal keenly and it had taken a long time to piece the business together. The fulfilling of orders was chaotic because the office had been ransacked and most papers destroyed, as well as stock losses. He wrote he was camping out in the farmhouse and would leave me to sort the house out on my return. What he did not tell me was that the couple in Sharon Cottage had parted because the husband had an affair but the rejected wife had also moved back to the farm.

Chapter 15
No Turning Back

Northern Rhodesia was still prosperous when we first lived there. Lusaka was a smart town and its mile long main street, Cairo Road, was shady, wide and dignified. Flowerbeds graced the tidy pavements and brilliantly blossomed flamboyant trees created an attractive central avenue. Side streets were dotted with jacaranda trees whose blossom drifted the pavements to create a deep mauve carpet in October and November. Colorful umbrellas shaded small tables on the lawn in front of the Dairy Produce Board and one could lunch on restaurant balconies or the pavement café on the corner. Smart shops catered for the expatriate population and the Africans were shunted round the back.

More than twenty years later in post independence Zambia, Lusaka, now the capital, was showing signs of an encroaching dilapidation. Some of it was due to the wear and tear of some else's war. True the small red brick hospital where our sons had been born was now the new U.T.H., the University Teaching Hospital and the University of Zambia stood proudly above the Great East Road on the way to the new International Airport. But on Cairo Road the pavement stones were broken, the flowerbeds were bare while Zambia's own people queued for staples such as oil, salt, soap, sugar and maize meal which was in very short supply. The pavement café had become a small supermarket but there was no flour on the shelves and bread was unofficially rationed in the rapidly changing circumstances. The outdoor market between Cairo Road's parallel streets had grown considerably and side streets were shabby with the over spill of vendors. The population had swelled as the people flocked to the line-of-rail towns and shanty townships sprawled for miles around the city, without the benefit of proper roads, electricity, sanitation or adequate water supply.

When Southern Rhodesia declared U.D.I., Unilateral Declaration of Independence, in a last ditch attempt to keep white supremacy, Zambia closed its border. Residents outside to the south were allowed back in, but all other traffic was suspended. I was on a brief holiday in S. Rhodesia at the time and such was the atmosphere at the border post when I returned, it was like hearing a prison door slam behind one. For S. Rhodesia the declaration of U.D.I. unleashed the dogs of a bitter civil war as the Shona and Matebele people of that region stepped up their fight against the white government.

For Zambia, who had always traded with, and indeed was dependent on the south, it was to initiate a time of an escalating cost of living, more shortages and real hardship. Zambia was landlocked, cut off from the port of Beira by the war in Mozambique, having long since lost her access to the western sea and Lobito Bay by a similar situation in Angola. There was no railway to East Africa and only a dirt road to the port of Dar-es-Salam. This road became the notorious "Hell Run", as enterprising private transporters large and small, attempted to in all that Zambia needed. Bad enough in the dry season, it was fifteen hundred miles of pure hell in the rains. Petrol became rationed and indeed, at one time petrol was actually air lifted from Elizabethville in the Congo. The supply of new vehicles and spare parts dried up and we had to use our vehicle tires down to the canvas and then patch the canvas.

For us the most difficult problems were shortage of animals' feed, agricultural and car spares, and fuel. After some time, the Chinese came in to build a railway from Dar-es-Salaam to Kapiri-Imposhi, a small town about a hundred miles north of Lusaka, where it met the Zambian rail system.

Thousands of Chinese workmen came to build this railroad and they were housed in large camps along the route. Many Christians longed for the opportunity to reach these people with the gospel, but the camps were guarded and the men never allowed in our towns except in supervised groups. Zambia paid for the railway by a trade agreement that meant our shops were flooded with Chinese goods. Happily for us they were cheap, fair quality and the foodstuffs very good.

The road to East Africa was finally tarred and things began to ease. Then came the over spill of Southern Rhodesia's fight for national independence and while the Shona leader Mugabe fought from behind the Mozambique lines, Joshua Nkomo's Matabele freedom fighters camped and trained inside our borders. Zambia's sympathetic President Kaunda allowed them first call on staple foodstuffs so matters did not improve for the ordinary Zambian people in this respect.

However towards the end of 1978 events brought matters to a climax. Strenuous efforts were made by all concerned which would ultimately allow the 1979 Commonwealth Conference to be held in Lusaka in July, albeit contingency plans were made in Nairobi, Kenya in case Lusaka was not safe. Things were beginning to calm down in the New Year and in February 1979 I made preparation to leave England and return to Zambia.

Gordon had told me he had hardly done a thing to the house, but I was totally unprepared for the shock that awaited me. Anxious to get home I was first surprised to see Pam with him at the airport, which gave us no privacy and that he insisted we call at the manse on the way back. He gave me no particular reason for this and I could not identify one. We just sat around and talked generally for an hour or so and the time dragged. I was tired after the flight from England and wanted to see Stuart.

When we finally arrived at the farm, it still bore all the outward marks of devastation but worse still, no attempt had been made to put the house ready for me. My bedroom was unprepared and evidence of Pam's occupancy was everywhere. Yet Gordon had known I was coming for some weeks.

Instead of the calm, thankful return I had looked forward to all that winter I was swept into a maelstrom of emotion and shock. Someone in need I had befriended and helped had become my husband's mistress. No amount of tears and pleas for forgiveness could banish the chill of that homecoming. I sat in the study rigid with pain while my room was cleaned, relieved only to know Stuart was lodging in town still. The day ended with me wondering how on earth could we go on from this.

Before sunrise I arose and walked in the freshness of a new day. It was the time of the horns, as our old Matebele herdsman had once told me; that first light when the herdsmen can just make out the shape of the horns in the cattle kraal against the predawn sky. Wet grass soaked my sandals and the hem of my dress as I walked to the river, a place I often sought in solitary prayer. I felt terribly tired and emotionally exhausted, overwhelmed and quite unable to formulate specific prayers. I just wanted to lean on the Lord and feel his arms round me till the pain subsided.

Turning from the waterfall, I walked up the lawns towards the road. The sun was rising up in a dazzling display to awaken the morning glories on the fence. The tips of plumed grass in the paddock were tinged with pink. Looking around, I thought about our early struggles, of what we had shared and seen of God's grace. I was very conscious of my own limitations. I was the product of a sheltered upbringing, schooled in a very conventional church. I did not see divorce as an option. It was against everything I believed in regarding Christian marriage. It was all very well for some to say it was acceptable in cases of adultery but for me, in reality, there were no such pat answers. That way lay certain destruction, of our personal lives, our family, our work, our witness. Had we lost all faith, all mercy, commitment, honor and integrity? No, I would not hurry down that path. Instead I would trust God to show me a better way. I would pray and believe that one day my husband would have the desire to get right with God. I was far too ignorant of the world then to realize, or even imagine that this was but the merest tip of the iceberg.

The sun rose above the horizon and from where I stood, the line of paw-

paw trees at the edge of the garden was in silhouette. Above them a skein of egrets, white against the clear sky, flew from the reed beds beyond the farm manager's house. I turned and went back to the house.

Immediately a few basic arrangements were made. Pam was driven to town. Her children were away at boarding school and the process of her own divorce was under way.

I forced my attention to restoring our home. There was so much to do, it helped me ride out the aftershock waves. Yet now and again, swift grief would attack me and I would sit, arms clasped about my body, rocking and silently weeping for lost dreams and impossible hopes. Yet, like the inner peace from God, which inevitably prevailed, the safety of my children and His very evident constancy gradually brought me round again to a renewed resolve to persevere.

I took stock of the mess that confronted me. Piled high in one shed was a complete miscellany of household goods, torn books, assorted broken furniture from the guest rooms, odd curtains, broken curtain rods, mattresses, cushions and blankets, rain soaked where the shed had leaked, even a rats nest or two. The sight put me in a militant mood that generated the energy I needed. This awful, stinking pile was a stark symbol of my life, but a great deal easier to get to grips with.

It was an enormous job, coming across things like some of my favorite pictures broken and stained with rainwater, a few remnants of our music collection with the tape pulled out and tangled, a handful of slides and snapshots of the children hopelessly damaged beyond repair. I hauled the lot outside and sorted through it. Some of it was re-usable once it was thoroughly cleaned. But there was still enough rubbish to keep a bonfire going for two days.

It was a month before an appreciable difference was made to the farmhouse. I was determined we would be clean and comfortable again despite our personal problems. There was nothing to be done about the damage to the floors, but mending, cleaning, and a load of white paint made a big difference to the interior. Chabaila worked wonders in repairs. Even when he made a new drawer to replace one missing from my desk, he carved the front to match the rest.

I spent days at the sewing machine I had brought from England. Some rooms such as the sitting room needed new curtains, but some odd ones from elsewhere, once clean were cut down and used for smaller windows. The sitting room and dining room furniture was mended, the gouges and scratches smoothed out, then they were re-stained and polished. Slowly and surely the house came to life.

Amazingly the sitting room carpet survived. Most of the upholstery bore marks of vandalism but this sort of damage was easy to deal with, it was the wounds of the heart that were difficult.

The authorities had advised us we must still not to go on our land across the river as a huge mopping-up exercise was now underway. Practically every blade of grass was turned over in an effort to make the area safe as preparations gained momentum for the Commonwealth Conference.

There were no visitors save one friend who came for a few nights while this mopping up was going on. The Zambian paramilitary forces were moving through the area, searching each property. They were well controlled and thorough, causing no damage but their presence was unsettling. Not knowing of their approach across our property, we went to town leaving our friend alone in the house for an hour or two.

When she saw the soldiers come up to the house she was so frightened she hurriedly shut herself inside a walk-in stationery cupboard. Terrified she heard the sound of heavy boots striding across the stone floor. The cupboard door opened and near fainting she heard a courteous voice say "Good morning, Madam. Why are you in the cupboard?

"I was frightened when I saw the soldiers," she whispered.

"No need to fear us, lady," the officer replied, probably aware she had every reason. He turned and went out, leaving her limp and rooted to the spot. Shortly afterward, he came back to tell her politely, they were leaving satisfied no ex-combatants lurked about undetected.

Curfews kept residents indoors while troops and others in authority moved around. Plans progressed for the Commonwealth Conference in Lusaka, at which the most urgent topic was to be Rhodesia/Zimbabwe, as the new territory was to be known.

After the farmhouse, I turned my attention to the guesthouses. Even if there were to be no more visitors, it was unbearable to see them in such a deplorable state. One by one I put them in good order. Doors were re-hung, windows mended, pieces picked from the remaining pile of damaged furniture and restored. I made some complete with new mattresses, lamps, drapes and covers, found mirrors and placed books. It was my own private war against such wanton destruction. Some were just scrubbed, painted and left empty for future renovation. By faith I worked and prayed, committing each room again for the Lord's use should it be needed, before moving on to the next. It was the first week in May when I finished the last one. Indeed it still required a final touch up on the paint, when I returned to the house to find seven people had arrived.

Their coming was a vindication of my hopeful labor yet, knowing the future was bound to be affected by our personal situation, I knew the mainspring was damaged. The outcome was not yet evident. Some would say, indeed they did afterwards, that we had no business attempting to serve the Lord with such problems. But of course I was only aware of the chasm in our marriage that I hoped would be healed. I had no knowledge, nor by the wildest stretch of imagination could I have envisaged what would be revealed later.

Nevertheless, while Gordon and I tried to salvage our relationship and get our lives on a new footing, a few people still continued to come to our door. Should we have turned them away? Those whom God touched seemed unaware of our problems. However imperfectly we functioned, God's grace to those people was evident and He had not abandoned us. I marveled when we were told of a Congolese Christian who, cycling along in the Katanga bush shortly before our raid, became convinced we were in danger. He did not know us or where we lived, but he received such a clear vision of our farm that when he told his fellow mission workers, the missionary recognized our place and they all gathered to intercede for us.

Could we rebuild, in faith and love for each other, let alone others? Could we again find a secure footing on a level path to the future, a straight way? Recent events had exposed gaps in our communication. I longed to see true repentance that might pave the way for reconciliation and renewal, but I could detect no change in him, no unbending. I could not entirely suppress my doubts though I hoped. Was it to be a false hope?

From now on, I could only answer for myself. I had chosen to return. There was no turning back. In England I had bravely answered the misgivings of my concerned family. From their security in prosperous, peaceful England, they had expressed grave doubts as to the wisdom of my decision, only in relation to the conditions in Zambia. If they had any other doubts or suspicions, they were not voiced.

How could I explain the 'rightness' of what I felt? Much as they loved me, they did not fully understand my commitment. I now found myself re-evaluating that same commitment. But in that I came round full circle. I had made my choice a long time ago, and though I was only too aware of a new vulnerability, my spirit was buoyed up by my recent experiences of God's grace.

PART 2

1980-1989

"But he said to me, my grace is sufficient for you; for my power is made perfect in weakness."
–2 Corinthians 12:9

Chapter 16
Brown Grass

Zambia in 1980 was a mixture of relief that the Rhodesian conflict was over, and the tussle to sort out the problems left in its wake. It was a huge exercise to repatriate the freedom fighters, round up the weaponry and repair the damage. Inevitably, in a situation where a gun could change hands for a few cigarettes, many arms filtered into local civilian hands. But for most of the expatriate population, it was just a matter of picking things up and getting on with our lives. However, for some it was not going to be quite the same again.

In Lusaka plans were going ahead for the Commonwealth Conference that would ultimately lead to the Lancaster House, London talks on Rhodesia/Zimbabwe. Just before the Commonwealth Conference when all Lusaka was preparing to welcome Queen Elizabeth II and the British Prime Minister Margaret Thatcher, we received page 2 of a letter from the British High Commission.

When Gordon showed it to me, it appeared to suggest that there was something to which we were invited. But we could not tell what. This page two spoke of 'hats and gloves optional' and 'lounge suits for men' etc. It was obviously the tail end of a letter setting the dress code for some function. Should the complete letter have come to us at all? Or was it a mistake?

Gordon took it with him to make inquiries at the High Commission. He came home with a proper invitation and page 1 of the letter. We were invited to a private reception to be held by Queen Elizabeth II at the British High Commission residence. It was to be held on the Sunday morning before the Conference began, and was for those British people in Zambia who had suffered during the hostilities.

Along with many others, we lined the path round the lawns while the Zambia Police Band played on the tennis court. The Queen walked slowly round clockwise, stopped every few paces for a brief greeting, Prince Phillip did the same counter-clockwise. Afterwards, we were ushered forward to be part of a smaller group presented to the Queen. Briefed with our names and a sentence encapsulating our experience, the Queen spoke a personal word to everyone in turn. When we were introduced, she said she had understood even our telephone line was out of order that day and "that must have been very difficult for you to get help." As I took her hand I was surprised by a palpable sense of awe, a combination of the sense of sovereignty she seemed to exude and my recognition of what she was. I was jolted by the awareness of all she represented. If this could be so strong in meeting such a small middle-aged lady, whatever is it going to be like when we meet Jesus!

For a short time after this we enjoyed a slightly more mellow time in our personal lives. One memorable evening Gordon and I walked, as we had often walked before, in harmony or so it seemed. At times like these it was easy to remember how it was in the early days. For a little time we could forget the differences that were pulling us apart and briefly enjoy the beauty of the night. As we had done so often in the past, we followed the circular drive that linked our houses. The great blue gum trees rustled gently above us and from the stock sheds there came small sleepy sounds and stirrings in the straw. Nothing marred the peace. And because there were no city lights or industrial pollution in the air, the high dark dome of heaven shone above us in all its starlit glory.

The warm evening air brought the sweet scent of citrus blossom drifting from the orchard. A bush baby's plaintive cry came from the wild fig tree beyond the dairy. I flashed my torch and caught its eyes reflected brightly for a moment. As we moved away our dog padded up and snuffled through the fence at the bullocks dozing under the cassia trees. Rounding the corner approaching the house, the sweet smell of datura, the moonflower, wafted around us from where its large creamy bells hung against the library wall. Down by the river, the trees looked dark and mysterious. Only the waterfall and the soft distant *hoo-hu, hoo-hu, hu-hu,"* call of a wood owl broke the silence.

The boys were home briefly so we had a holiday together with Grace who had decided to remain in Zambia. We piled our gear into the pick-up truck and headed for the Luangwa Valley. It was approximately 400 miles to Chipata, then we struck north to the South Luangwa River.

The long journey was made more tedious by military roadblocks. Although we had been forced to learn to live with these for years, I was never at ease and disliked them intensely. Gordon however, was never at a loss. The soldiers understandably got bored stuck out on the road, miles from anywhere and were often a bit edgy. Like many other travelers we took along newspapers, booklets and tracts to ease the way. Cigarettes were a favored gift, but we did not carry any. However, whatever we did offer was usually received well.

But all minor irritations were forgotten once we arrived. Our camp overlooked the river. Set among large shady trees, the open fronted dining area gave us a spectacular view of a lagoon. We could watch elephants drink as we breakfasted, pick out the flash of a diving kingfisher or the submarine glide of a darter as we lazily lunched, binoculars always at the ready.

On arrival we handed our supplies to the camp cook who would prepare all our meals. Our days settled into a pattern. Shortly after dawn, with the sun scarcely risen, we would leave the river and drive into the bush. As the dry season progresses, the tall grass thins out and the waterholes diminish. Now it was August, and the game were slowly concentrating towards the river. When we returned to the camp some two or three hours later, the smell of fresh baked bread greeted us and we fell onto our breakfast with deep satisfaction. Lazing through the heat of the day, we would sally forth late in the afternoon as the bush stirred to life, to return in the dusk, replete with pleasure, to recount our day's adventures and thrills over a hearty supper while we watched the moon rise over the river.

Our days were filled with a dozen delights. One night we stood at the doorway of our hut. In the moonlight, we could see a rhino munching fruit pods. The massive animal was only about fifteen feet away. We watched hundreds of lovely Carmine bee-eaters in the sand cliffs above the river. And we found great delight as a flock of Nyasa lovebirds suddenly took off in a cloud of color. We laughed to see rafts of hippo frolicking in the lagoons and later we had a real fright when, after trailing an elephant for a while, it suddenly turned round and charged our truck. Gordon swiftly reversed, straight into an anthill, and we experienced an electrifying few moments before, pale faced and sweating, we crashed out over some tree roots and through some small bushes and finally got away.

All too soon the holidays were over. Stuart went to England for further studies and Grace decided on a secretarial course at Lusaka College of Further Education, while life on the farm settled into its usual routine. Nevertheless, in general it had been a difficult year. The upsets and setbacks of the preceding months had left a painful legacy, and the economic and climatic conditions in the country only compounded the struggle.

The slate gray ribbon of road unfolded before me in the early morning sunlight. The air was fresh but it would not last. My passenger, the anxious wife of one of our workers, was cradling a sick child. Later I would take them to the hospital. The vehicle was laden with produce to be delivered. A shopping list and details of a spare part needed was on the dashboard.

Nearly two hours later I was stuck in traffic. He had said not to be late and here I was crawling up the Leopard's Hill Road feeling cross with myself for not avoiding this route. It was not easy to forget that maybe there would be hold-ups here, but knowing my husband needed the car back as early as possible, I had only remembered this short cut from the hospital to my final

125

destination. Fool! I banged my hand on the steering wheel in frustration and then felt guilty. I would do better to thank God it was not my family trailing to the cemetery.

AIDS had tightened its hold on the land. It was becoming commonplace to see vans and trucks driving with their headlights full on, carrying a coffin and loaded with mourners. Zambian custom demanded that oncoming traffic should stop and pull over while the sad cavalcade passed. I had already done this twice on my way into town that morning. Whenever I heard the mourners' dirge, it never failed to trigger tremors of sympathy for their plight. How stark was the contrast between them and the sleek silent limousines and dark funereal clothes of the wealthy.

Finally I was past the cemetery gates and able to put my foot down. My errand over, I thankfully left the overheated city and took the road home. A column of white smoke rose high to the south where a bush fire raged outside the city limits. The road was rough with un-mended potholes and I entered our gates with a sigh of relief. Twice I had passed small fires where the dry grass verge was burning. Where previous fires had passed I saw long vistas of utterly dry dusty land. The ground resembled brown cracked concrete.

Gordon was standing under the shade of the blue gums on the drive. He flagged me down and dismissed the worker he had been talking to.

"I've been waiting, you're late Anne," without the preamble of greeting, his words sounded more like an accusation.

"Sorry, I got delayed," He brushed aside my attempts at an explanation. "Just give me the keys. Did you get the part?"

"Yes," I reached into the car, grabbed my bag and gave him the car keys. "Did you want the it now?"

"No, drop it off at the workshop on your way down. I'll see you later." With that he turned the car and was off.

Perhaps I was unreasonable, but knowing he was worried and rushed did not help. Ever since my fateful homecoming after our brush with the war the previous year, the strain between us, which we could nearly forget when things were going well, was all too often perilously near the surface, the veneer transparent in times of stress. The strain of this difficult year was showing. We no longer shared fellowship because he shied off and avoided facing any personal issue, totally refusing to be in any way accountable.

Our pick-up truck was stolen. We could not replace it. There was none to be had. Everyday presented new logistical problems. I refused to succumb to the idea that problems were worse in Africa. It just seemed that way some day, especially when they crowded in day after day, hitting us in bunches.

Walking down to the house, I gave myself up to the simple pleasure of admiring the towering poinsettias. Their magnificent dinner plate size heads of scarlet bracts reared up against a cloudless blue sky of such intensity, the feast of color was almost too much for ones eyes to bear.

The lawns showed brown patches among the dun seeded grass. Formerly there had always been enough water to irrigate these, and to spare, but now only essential needs such as stock and marketable crops had call on that precious commodity. Somehow this dry season had seemed twice as long, and more than twice as tiring. Our problems seemed larger and the solutions became more elusive. Gordon said little apart from conventional conversation. Except when he was absent, I had little to do with the running of the farm now. My stamina and willpower was finite. At times it was all I could do to fight the doubts that sometimes crowded in.

Was I a fool to go on hoping and praying for renewal? How much of the present deadlock was my fault? Should I be doing things differently? I knew once I allowed my doubts and fears to get the upper hand, it would not only not bring a solution, but would dissipate my energy further. Resolutely I put counter productive thoughts aside and tried to concentrate on the tasks in hand.

Across the road, a mulberry hedge bordered the top field. Its deep green luxuriant leaves stood out fresh in the dusty atmosphere. A long stretch of it had been layered to form a thick impenetrable barrier against livestock. The rest was growing free, reaching some 8-10 feet high. Recently, stock feed had been in such short supply we had been forced to harvest this bounty and feed it to the milking herd together with chopped up banana leaves. We mixed this green stuff with straw from the floor of the deep litter poultry house. This litter was valuable for the amount of poultry meal that was dropped from the feeders. The milk yield kept up reasonably well so once more we got through a crisis.

The work of God was still going on, but slowly. A church had become established across the river and we had found a young Zambian man to take care of that. But there were few visitors apart from an occasional overland expedition. Military mopping up activities were tailing off and occasional curfews still reminded us of the war, but most of us were trying hard to forget it.

Food shortages of all sorts were now the norm. Prices rocketed as inflation cut deep. Good housekeeping meant learning to keep one's ear to the ground to detect supplies arriving at various points round the town, furious telephoning round the alert one's friends, and queues. I became adept at gathering supplies from afar, even as far off as South Africa and England. Hardly anyone traveled without a list of what to look for or track down.

Among the farmers barter became fashionable again. What tiny amount of flour was available in the country went direct to bakers to keep them in business, but bread was in very short supply. I rationed bread to one meal per day, and hoarded a little flour for the rare treat of an occasional birthday cake. This treasure had to be kept in the freezer to keep it free of weevils. I experimented with homemade cereals, using sun dried fruit, oats brought in by friends from South Africa and local groundnuts.

It was nearly the end of October. Leaving the litter of lunch preparation on the table, I went to the kitchen door and stared out. It was abnormally hot and as I looked towards the river, I wondered if the weirs would hold up until it rained. Though we had the water rights over the head of the river, we were naturally obliged to make sure a sufficient supply flowed down river for our neighbors.

Yesterday, the limit had been reached and we were forced to stop pumping early in the day. It would take almost a full day for the weir pools to fill. From now on we could take the bare minimum for our stock and hope the rains came before the water vanished.

The previous two seasons had been drier than usual. The growth of the city, whose official limits now came within a few miles of the farm, had reduced the water table to ten feet below what it was when we first came to our property. It was very serious and owing to the setbacks in our business since the war, there was no spare money to sink a well. A great deal was riding on our hopes for a good rainy season.

Storm clouds were piling up to the north. Great gray towers that promised so much, but as yet withheld the promised bounty. Perspiration trickled down my back and I pushed straggling damp hair off my face and sighed. A vivid slash of lightning shot among the clouds, followed by a muted distant rumble of thunder. It was miles away and here everything still wilted under the brassy noon sky and the sun's relentless glare.

Down in the garden I saw our old gardener unhurriedly going through the motions. I smiled to myself. He was working his way toward the flowerbed where he had surreptitiously planted a dagga plant or two. Did he think we had not noticed? He glanced at the sky, and obviously deciding it was lunch break time, wandered off and flopped down in the shade of the jacaranda tree. I watched him rummage in a tattered pocket for his habitual bit of snuff, lift it from his palm with gnarled fingers and take a luxurious sniff and he lay back in contentment. For a moment I quite envied him. If only my problems would yield to such a simple remedy. He was a faithful old man though long overdue for retirement but we had no desire to deny him the dignity of a job while he could still manage the flower garden.

All morning echoes of past fear had drifted unbidden through my mind. They were less prevalent now the further my experiences of the previous year slipped behind. Nevertheless, from time to I did remember the massacre of the Elim missionaries in S. Rhodesia a few months prior to our raid and the subsequent incidents and deaths in our own neighborhood. No doubt those Christians, as had many others, prayed for protection in similar situations. Why had we been spared? I was everlastingly grateful, but there was no room for complacency. I was not particularly brave, no more than the next woman, but in God's grace those fears subsided as I reminded myself of the Holy Spirit's enabling power to meet whatever the need, and once again my peace was reinstated.

Two days later the rains broke. A new breath of life flowed over the land. I stood under the eaves as the rain sluiced off the roof like a waterfall. Throughout the garden leaves gleamed as the dust rinsed away and the air bore a hundred new fragrances. For the moment my problems dissolved under the precious onslaught.

Chapter 17
The Camp

With the onset of the rains we all felt revived. The business was going fairly well and Gordon appointed a Zambian Agricultural College graduate as his assistant. During the previous dry season we had been better able to assess the damage to our buildings across the river. Now we could consider the future of our investment there.

The buildings on this land comprised what remained of our Campsite. Some very basic repairs were possible but there was no spare money available. They had been used on two occasions as temporary housing for missionary families who had been forced to leave their homes in Katanga Province, Zaire, at a time of political unrest and danger. Most of the equipment and simple furniture had been stolen, so we left the remaining doors locked and decided the whole complex must stay closed until such time as we could continue.

Originally the land opposite our homestead had been set aside for the possible future development of our missionary work. For several years we had not seen the precise use it could be used for, so we waited. But even through the difficult years of re-establishing ourselves after losing our home by fire, we clung to the hope that the day would come when the door would open for something specific.

Early in 1970 it had come to our notice that an interdenominational group of people in Lusaka were actively seeking a site on which to hold camps for young people, seminars and conferences and such like. The first indication was the need being made known as a prayer request in our church in the town.

For a long time, though we had no money of our own to spare, we had been on the lookout for an opportunity to open up our land for further Christian outreach. Ever since our arrival, we had believed that the land directly opposite the homestead would be suitable. Like the land on which our home and farm buildings were situated, it sloped down to the river in a series of natural terraces, with many fine trees and grassy slopes.

When we heard of this need, we therefore, spoke up and offered the use of this land, inviting this group to come and view it if they were interested. As it happened another piece of land was offered a few miles away by another Christian family, at about the same time.

In due course, the interested group arranged to view both sites. Afterwards, it was always a matter of encouragement that there was a choice at this time, because when the group accepted our site, Gordon and I felt it was confirmation of our hopes and dreams for such a project.

However, this selection committee was not in a position to finance any development themselves; they were first and foremost concerned that there 'be' such a place. But the open door that their acceptance represented to us after the years of waiting, was a 'green light' enough. Talks with the group produced ideas of how this site could be utilized. There was only one other such site in the country, on the Copperbelt, so they felt it was important that such a site be developed near the capital, in Zambia's Central Province.

It was suggested that in the main, the site could be used for organizations such as Scripture Union that was strong in Zambia in many schools. Also that other missions and church groups may well use it for training sessions, as well as groups such as Nurses Christian Fellowship and the Evangelical Fellowship of Zambia. Indeed there were many opportunities for all sorts of people to enjoy using the site. In time all of this happened and the camp became an asset to much Christian endeavor.

Within a month the first gift of money was given and although small, kept up the momentum of interest in the new project. A roadway was cleared so that campsite would have its own access directly off the main road, which was about a mile past the turn off to the farm. The project was well publicized in the churches and offers of help soon came in, particularly from our own church where there was a large student body from the colleges and University.

It was at a gathering of young people from the Brethren Church who had spent an afternoon at the farm, that the meeting took place between a young German volunteer who was teaching in Lusaka at the Trades Training Institute, and a shy, clever young accountant. Kris had come forward very early on. He was a civil engineer, and started off by surveying the site and searching our land for any natural resources, sand and gravel etc. He rigged up an extension light so he could work late into the evenings. He made the first experimental concrete blocks, designed the first houses and made models to interest others on the project.

Kris had asked us if he could live at the farm in order to make it easier for him to give more time to the project and this proved to be a very happy arrangement. Pete was the accountant and the two young men talked a long time. It became obvious that Pete was very interested. But neither said anything to us that day. The first intimation that the duo had formed a working partnership came later in the week. Pete, very correct in his business suit, arrived straight from work complete with briefcase. He walked straight into the house without a word and headed towards Kris' room, only to appear a little later in old shorts, a battered hat and clutching a shovel. The animated pair headed for the campsite without a backward look.

Having Pete to work alongside him tremendously encouraged Kris. When he finally left Zambia to return to Germany, Pete moved into his room. He brought great enthusiasm and business acumen to the project in addition to his labors. Then another young civil engineer, Mac, got involved and the work went on a pace. Both these men met their future wives among the young Christians in Lusaka during this period and later Mac's wedding also took place on the farm.

Working parties became a regular event. The dry season was excellent for building for the weather was so stable. The need was made known in the student body and our farm vehicle would collect a group of willing workers at college or university campus on Saturday mornings. On the site everyone pitched in, dug, shoveled, wheeled barrows, carried water or manned the concrete mixer that was a most welcome acquisition, courtesy of Mac. Our children of course, were generally underfoot and the sounds of all this activity floated across the river and often attracted some of our visitors to pitch in as well.

Then in the afternoon, hungry tired and jolly it was time to swim in the river and flop down on the lawns, to enjoy hamburgers and cool drinks. Someone would fetch a guitar and often, as darkness fell, we would sing round a bonfire. Then everyone would clamber on board the truck for the trip back to town. They were busy and joyous days.

The project was named 'Evangelical Outreach'. Cash was slow to come in but progress was steady. Sometimes we could help a little with skilled labor from the farm. There proved little building material of real use on the land, so most supplies were bought as money came in. However, we found some slate for the verandas and some stone for ornamental walls and steps. Our farm vehicles were used to haul concrete blocks, sand, cement and later door and window frames, though our farm carpenter made some on site.

The first houses were of three rooms each with a veranda. Then two large buildings were put up to serve as dormitories and another building for meetings that was also to house a library. There were two ablution blocks. This gave the camp flexibility. A dining hall and chapel were planned for the future.

It was planned that the camp be used in the dry season only i.e. Easter to October. This meant that meals could be taken outside under the shade of the trees, on a grassy slope outside the kitchen. The iron rim of a car wheel, suspended in a tree and struck with an iron bar, was a simple and effective gong that also announced meetings. This central area was also the site of the campfire, round which fellowship and music were enjoyed.

The ground sloped towards the river and all the buildings had been built on the contour, no-one overlooking another. They all faced the river with steps, owing to the fall of the land, which were popular sitting places. Care was taken to preserve the lovely indigenous trees. The site being rested in the rainy season also enabled it to be kept in good condition.

A lady who taught Hotel Management skills, the wife of a Lusaka pastor, worked out food quantities for various large numbers of many popular camp menus. These, with other helpful suggestions and information were typed and put into leaflet form and made available to camp organizers and cooks.

Until such time as there would be a permanent manager living on site as we hoped, all the equipment was kept in a store at the farm, except the industrial cooking stove. I looked after the equipment and issued it at the start of each camp. Mattresses, cooking pots, dishes, cutlery, benches, tables and chairs, brooms, and cylinder of bottled gas for the big gas stove. Campers brought their own food, bedding and cleaning materials, also their own cooks. The cost to campers was kept low to place the whole facility within the reach of as many people as possible, particularly students. As the years went by and costs inevitably rose, this intention was adhered to and for several years the real cost of using the site was not raised and we subsidized the project thereafter.

The first phase of the campsite could sleep up to one hundred youngsters, sleeping dormitory fashion on mattresses on the floor. Often when camps were in progress, the sound of singing wafted across the river to the farm. The traffic between farm and the camp was constant. The river was used for swimming below the water pump and for baptismal events. A year or so after the project commenced, a large area was cleared to one side and a sports field was established. "Tiyende ku caya bala", the shout would ring out, "Let's play football."

Often campers erected tents to house family parties and occasionally a large marquee was added for a large camp. On one memorable occasion, three hundred people built grass walled 'stockades' each with a central fireplace and slept under the stars.

Throughout the years of unrest and war, we had struggled to keep our telephone working. Now we invested in a new telephone. The 30ft high radio mast had only just been put up and the new service initiated when a call came through when Gordon was away for the day. It was the United Nations High Commission for Refugees in Lusaka. We were well acquainted with their personnel, having been involved in several instances. The caller needed our help.

Apparently a refugee camp, only a few miles to the south of the city, had been bombed that morning and it was necessary to evacuate more than eighty of the uninjured Angolan refugees without delay. Cluster bombs had been dropped and the place was a shambles. U.N.H.C.R. would provide blankets and food, together with supervisors.

"My husband isn't here," I replied.

"It's really urgent, Mrs. Bland. The Salvation Army do not have the space. We think your place is more suitable." I went quiet for a moment, wishing Gordon were around to take the responsibility, agree or refuse. I knew what he meant. Our camp, being well out of town, and therefore more easily isolated, was the most suitable as the situation was politically sensitive, I snapped back to attention as the voice came again on a higher note.

"What do you say, Mrs. Bland?" The voice now had an edge. Then came the clincher. "Two thirds of them are women and children."

"How soon do you want to come?" I asked.

"E.T.A. in about an hour and a half. Thanks," and he rang off. I put the phone down, with a whispered prayer. I had a sick feeling in my stomach. I took the campsite keys from their hook, grabbed a bag of sugar, and a packet of tea from the kitchen and ran to the store where remnants of the camp equipment were kept. There was no vehicle handy. I shouted across the field to summon the nearest farm workers. My tone brought them on the run.

Swiftly, I summoned the tractor driver to couple up the trailer and bade the men as quickly as possible. Thankfully, there was a large, full, cylinder of bottled gas. As I urged the men, I ticked off my mental list of what was needed, of what we had available. The U.N.H.C.R. representative had made a strong suggestion that neither our workers, nor myself, should be directly involved - it was not desirable that we should be there once their people arrived with their charges. I was happily to comply. Time was of the essence, and I hurried the men.

Once the tractor was headed for the cattle crossing over the river, I followed. I called at the dairy on the way, ordering the cowman to bring a gallon of milk to the camp without delay. While the men unloaded the stuff onto the veranda of the first house, I opened up the kitchen and laid the keys to the other buildings on the table, flanked by the tea, sugar and milk. I sent one man quickly to switch on the water pump and check the tanks were full, while all the others were instructed to return to the farm with the tractor.

As I filled the tea urn, I prayed for the refugees in their trauma. I wanted to be able to bid them welcome, but knew I should not stay. It was not necessary, or wise. I turned the urn to 'low' and left the camp. As I crossed the stepping-stones across the river back to my house, I heard the refugees' truck pull in.

Chapter 18
The Hidden Snare

"But he said to me, "my grace is sufficient for you, for my power is made perfect in weakness."
–2 Corinthians 12:9

Life in Zambia was slowly restored to normal but it would never be as before. Regrettably there were many weapons left behind or cheaply traded. This ushered in a period that was characterized by an increase of armed robberies. At one school, a mother who had come to collect her child was shot dead when she protested instead of immediately handing over her car keys at gunpoint. A similar incident took place in our neighborhood. In town people built security walls round their property.

These walls were usually built of concrete blocks, some 6-8ft high, topped with broken glass. This meant the employment of a guard/watchmen on the gate, usually with dogs. But these precautions then became a danger as people were sometimes held up and robbed as they waited in their vehicles for their watchmen to open the gates.

When Grace decided to stay in Zambia, and subsequently trained as a legal secretary, she began a youth group in the Salvation Army hall. She had a particular interest in reaching young people in the town from several different cultural backgrounds, many of whom she had first known at school. This group, of which several came to Christ, later integrated into churches in Lusaka.

Zambia and Rhodesia/Zimbabwe were still sorting out a few problems, not least of which was rehabilitation of the thousands of freedom fighters. A large portion of these young men had been forcibly bussed from their villages as children and grown up in the camps, only taught their propaganda, to use weapons and kill. There was one last curfew very hurriedly imposed in October 1980. We had planned an evening barbecue to celebrate Grace's 21st birthday and we had to cancel at less than 24 hours notice. Our telephone was out of order, so we could not contact our guests. It was cancelled as no one could travel to or from town in the evening. But not daunted, the guests came, in small groups all daylong instead of all at once as planned and by nightfall just the family and the residents on the farm enjoyed the barbecue under the stars.

The farm manager's house was not needed for the new farm assistant. Instead he was housed in the small flat above the garage and Bethesda house was put in order and let to a young couple with two children, who were friends of ours, and with whom we had enjoyed fellowship over several years.

When Gordon decided we should have a holiday in England in the spring of 1981 I was delighted. But, because he did not want to leave his young assistant in sole charge for long, he decided I should go first for a few weeks. He would then join me for a week or so, after which I would return to look after things. I accepted because I wanted the chance to see my family and the boys. However, in my absence, his avowed contrition after the debacle involving Pam following our raid, was put to test. It failed miserably.

As I breakfasted on the plane, the African sunrise streaked the sky orange, gold and lemon. I had no expectation that I was returning to anything other than the usual farming problems. My, but it felt good to be coming home. I loved the overnight flight, that little space between two worlds. Saying goodbye to my family as the sun set on scenes of my former life was always a bit sad. But waking in a new dawn speeding back to the land of my adoption and the work I loved always filled me with contentment.

We began our descent and as the undercarriage clunked down, I could see more clearly the vast expanse of brown grass and felt again the familiar rush or affection for this land. As the earth rushed up, I felt the ground effect cushion our impact. I head the touchdown 'squeak' as the tires met the runway and we rumbled to a halt. I breathed a brief thanksgiving prayer and unbuckled my seatbelt.

My luggage cart sped away in the charge our driver and I followed him to the car park. Crossing the tarmac I lifted my face to breeze and was greeted again with the familiar 'ping-ping' wind snap of the halyards against the flagpoles lining the airport approach. We drove down the Great East Road towards the city and I reflected on the week just passed. Our plans had not worked quite as smoothly as anticipated. Gordon confirmed my return flight and took me to the airport, only to find the flight had left two hours previously. Sure enough, when I took the ticket from him and checked it was correct. I had accepted his word when he said we should leave for the airport. It was a complete anti-climax having to trail back for another two days and I was dismayed that I could not be pleased that we had two more days together. It did not occur to me that this small delay would have any significance.

We skirted the city and sped out to Lusaka West. We turned off the tar road and down the last half -mile or so of sand road. As we passed through the farm gate and I saw the cattle grazing beneath the blue gum trees I was excited all over again. At the end of the drive, the car turned the last corner by the house, and I caught a glimpse of the waterfall glinting in the sun, framed in fronds of golden-shower creeper. The dogs rushed out as the driver tooted and stopped. I was home.

Within an hour I was faced with difficulties in the office as our secretary had walked out in dubious circumstances. She had left a message to say that although she had originally intended to stay until I arrived, she had decided to just go when advised of my delay. She was the daughter of missionary friends and had previously played an important role in the ministry, so I was very concerned. I could not understand her leaving, but more particularly why she should go without waiting to see me. However, hard on the heels of this unwelcome news was even more unsettling tidings.

Our young farm assistant, whom we had accepted as a Christian had been drunk on several occasions, twice beating his wife and even now she was in hospital as a result. I began to think things were falling apart. But worse was to follow. Our young friend, the tenant from Bethesda, came down to speak to me. In a painful interview, he told me about my husband's determined and quite improper visits to his wife. There was no mistake, there were witnesses to blatant wrongdoing. Reluctantly I had to accept that they would move. I could only share his distress and sadly see them go. After being friends for ten years, it was a grievous loss.

By the end of the week it seemed I had never been away, except now I was two valued friends and colleagues short. Some time later they went overseas and my saddened spirit sank to a new low. When I confronted Gordon about this he rationalized his behavior and became very angry. In no way would he be accountable.

Sometime before this, Gordon had moved from our church in town and, with the help of two young Zambian church members commenced services in one of the suburbs in order to build a church there under the umbrella of the established church. He made it clear he expected me to go with him. Then began another very difficult time for me. After a while, I realized he was again spending time with Pam. About that time I discovered some pornographic material hidden in the office and confronted Gordon. He retaliated with physical anger, knocking me across the room with enough force to break my glasses. This frightened me, and I began to dread his sudden mood changes.

Previously, I had gone to the church leadership about his infidelity, but I think they had difficult believing me. After all he was one of their Deacons and his apparent sincerity and personal charisma carried the day. Moreover

I knew him to be a master at dissembling. I later learned that the Pastor was very uneasy and continued to be suspicious, but did not take any action then. Ostensibly, Gordon carried on.

Only recently recovered from a bout of amoebic dysentery, another health problem began to plague me. My deepening anxieties were having a debilitating effect. The accidental discovery of pornographic material among my husband's things sent me on a hunt through the study, library and house and, in his absence one day I had a good bonfire. I knew deep in my heart I could not clean up someone else's mess, but my revulsion demanded some action. He never challenged me about their disappearance and when I brought the subject up, denied their existence to my face.

I embarked on spiritual warfare, combat that lasted for years. I would not tolerate such a wicked invasion of my life and my home. I did not fully understand then that these things were but symptoms of a far deeper disorder. At times it seemed as if I was attacked on all sides. It was not my overwrought imagination. One afternoon, my laundry worker brought the basket of clean linen to me as usual. When I prepared to stow the linen in the linen cupboard, I leapt back in terror. A puff adder was coiled between the folded sheets.

Confrontation with Gordon proved futile. He rationalized his behavior, angrily accusing me of being domineering and prudish. On the day I found out his relationship with Pam was continuing, my anger, frustration and anxiety reached an explosive level. I felt I would fly into a thousand pieces. I managed to hang on until I saw him walk down towards the river. I followed him.

"Gordon, wait. I must talk to you," I began as I caught up with him.

"What about, can't it wait?"

"No, it can't," I replied, striving for control. He was still walking.

"Be quick then, I'm going to the cattle dip." He stood there and looked at me without interest or expression. I took a deep breath.

"I know you've been seeing Pam," I began. "Why do you persist in one act publicly, and be quite different in private? Why do you break every promise you've made to me?" Despite my efforts to keep calm, my voice was rising.

"What are you talking about?" He turned angrily to face me.

"I know you are still seeing her. Don't deny it, you've been seen."

"What do you know about it?" He snapped back. I gasped at his obduracy. His stony face frightened me, but I tried again.

"Why do you say one thing and do another?" I was beginning to tremble.

"So what's got to do with you? I'm my own master. I will not be dictated to," his face took on the ugly look I hated so much.

"What's it got to do with me? You carry on living in this double standard manner, showing one face to the church and those who look up to you. You're so different to your family." In my helpless rage I spluttered to a stop.

"You're hysterical. Stop this stupid shouting." His implacable coldness was like hitting a stone -wall. I began to cry, wringing my hands in distress. He went, "For goodness sake, pull yourself together." But I was past caring.

"You're a real wolf in sheep's clothing. You've got me over a barrel. You know I'm not well, but you don't care at all, do you? I was pacing back and forth in my agitation. "You just go on doing whatever you want. Why do you want to look big in front of others and ignore the love and respect your family would give you if only you'd stop doing these things. Why don't you practice what you preach?" I ran out of steam and stood gasping, tears pouring down my face.

"Stop this puritanical tirade. I'm your husband. I'll do what I want, and how I want. Don't let me hear any more of this dramatic nonsense. I'm responsible before God, so shut up. And stop blubbering," he finished irritably and strode off.

He really does think it's okay, I thought in frightened astonishment. So be it. Afterwards, I was thankful we had been out of sight of the house and probably out of earshot too. It was becoming more and more difficult to manage when other folk were so often around us. How would it all end?

Almost no one came to visit us now, which was not surprising. There were however, a few missionary friends passing through from time to time. A mixed-marriage refugee couple from South Africa came to us while waiting for U.N.H.C.R. to arrange their passage to Brazil; and after them, a stranded Australian lady and her three children.

On the day I went into the hospital in Lusaka, there was still the remnants of underlying tension abroad. Medicines and medical equipment was patently in short supply. I had been advised to report at 6 am, ready for day surgery. When we arrived we found the hospital gates heavily guarded and no private vehicles allowed in. So Gordon dropped me outside the gates and I walked the rest of the way in my dressing gown. Just as well it was not raining.

That afternoon as I sleepily recovered, I looked around the ward. A 'pinky', the ward maid who wore a pink uniform overall, was sweeping the floor in a desultory fashion. She ended up with a small pyramid of dust in the middle of the room. I watched as she looked around for something to use in lieu of a dustpan. She moved towards me, took the clipboard from the end of my bed, brushed up the dirt and threw it out of the nearest window. Casually giving the board a swipe against her pink rump to clean it off, she solemnly returned it to the foot of my bed. I smiled. Somehow that humorous little tableau lightened my heart, for the moment.

Once fully recovered, I began to think of leaving again, but the practicalities, to me, were fraught with difficulties. I had no money, no alternative place to go. Grace was now working as a legal secretary, temporarily house-sitting in town with a friend. In England, the boys were in lodgings. My brother was already caring for my mother. It was not possible to set up alternative accommodation for myself locally in Zambia, and in any case, it would not work. It was time of great emotional confusion as I struggled with the enormity of my dilemma.

Deep down, I knew I had to make a change, for God is not the author of confusion. I did not believe it was His will that my life was being reduced to naught in this manner, nor was it pleasing Him that our family and all we had believed in, and worked for should so disintegrate. But God's word also says *"Depart, depart, go out from there! Touch no unclean thing! Come out from it and be pure..." Isaiah 52 verse 11*. The following verse also carries the promise of His provision and care in such a situation. But before I could make plans the opportunity was lost.

Chapter 19
A Portentous Letter

Gordon announced he was going away, and in a matter of days he was off to England. This had become an increasing defense pattern. Unwilling to be accountable, he would go off at short notice, to the bush, to friends, to England "on business", leaving me the responsibility of the farm. Not that I was unable to handle this, indeed I was very capable; but it tied my hands. Despite a certain relief in the respite from personal strife his absence afforded me, I was still committed to the belief that it was possible for our marriage to be healed if only he would face the problem, confess the sin and ask God to help him. Whatever my outward demeanor communicated to those around me, I began a deep personal pilgrimage. Deeply convinced that God was able to rebuild our lives, I struggled with my own accountability in the situation.

Before he left, we shared a few rare, precious moments when he took me aside and confessed he believed he had two demons with him since childhood. In tears he begged me to pray for him, which I willingly did then and there. I had long known he had many difficulties in his childhood but I had no knowledge of any possible ramifications. It was totally outside of my experience.

After we talked, I laid hands on him and commanded the spirits to leave in Jesus' Name, he gagged and retched and then keeled over. I opened all the windows and sat beside him praying quietly. After a while he recovered. I suggested, since we had been on our own, that we drive into town and share all this with the pastor, and he agreed. To what extent the pastor was experienced in these matters, I could not tell, but as we left after a brief prayer, I was left still deeply concerned, and could only pray this would prove to be a real turning point.

This exceptional interlude refueled my desire to leave no stone unturned in seeking a healing. Shortly after Gordon left, I sought an opportunity to consult the only person I knew of in the territory with the right experience. He was several hundred miles away, two days journey. There was a degree of difficulty involved, because I did not want to divulge to anyone else the true reason for my trip, and I did not think it wise to travel so far on my own in case of a breakdown. I waited on the Lord for an opening and put out a few feelers. One large mission headquarters in the city wanted to get a consignment of X-ray plates to their hospital some seven hundred miles away, comparatively close to where I wanted to go.

Fortunately at this time we had a couple staying on the farm who were very helpful. The gentleman agreed to go with me while his wife looked after my household. We broke our journey on the Copperbelt overnight, and pushed on to our destination the following day. The gentleman did the lion's share of the driving over hundred of miles of corrugated dirt road and his company was a blessing. The morning after we arrived, I sent him on with the X-ray plates to the hospital, and I spent the day alone with my host and his wife, who received me very graciously. Before I left, it was agreed Gordon and I would be invited to a missionary gathering to be held later that year at their station. I was to do everything I could to persuade my husband to take me there.

Immediately heartened, I returned to the farm. When my husband returned, we talked about this and he agreed to take me back there to talk and receive ministry. Accordingly we made the trip a few weeks later in September. The situation had eased somewhat between us, and I had high hopes. We both enjoyed the general fellowship and our host, true to his word, took care to spend time privately with Gordon who opened up to a remarkable degree. Our host then specifically instructed him what to do, referring to what is taught in Luke 11:20-26. For example, he must clean out any remaining pornography, to walk the farm, with witness, in repentance and obedience, claiming back any area given over to the enemy, to do everything to ensure that the enemy (Satan) had no further foothold. We journeyed home in harmony feeling much better.

However, after our return, I was dismayed there was no immediate sign of him doing any of this. Knowing he had to do it himself, I sought the Lord but put no pressure on him. But as the weeks went by, my heart sank as I wondered what effect this would have on our future.

During October and November we were plagued by several thefts. By Christmas there had been a dozen or so incidents, stock theft, large and small, break-ins to house and guest-cottages, another of our vehicles went.

On Christmas Eve, I drove the farm van to town, taking eggs and cream to a friend. Shortly after turning onto the approach to the city, I felt something akin to a push between my shoulder blades that caused me to swerve. The van crossed two traffic lanes without colliding with another vehicle and hit the concrete base of a street- light at about 40 miles per hour. At no time did I blackout, and actually got myself out of the van, to fall on my knees on the grass verge. The almost new van was a "write-off." I had suffered damaged ribs, a sprained thumb, and a nasty bang on my head where it had connected with the rear-view mirror. I also had a deep slash in my left knee from a sliver of metal. I was also streaming blood from my nose, enough to soak my dress that was also covered in spilt cream and broken eggs.

A passer-by stopped and took me to my doctor. She stitched my knee and gave me some basic injections, then arranged transport for me to the University Teaching Hospital for X-rays. Because the telephone at the farm was not working that day, the gentleman who took me to my doctor, then offered to drive out to the farm with a message. Gordon caught up with me at the hospital where the X-rays had revealed a couple of cracked ribs only. I was allowed home, extremely thankful not to be in the hospital for Christmas.

By the time I got home some five hours later the broken eggs, spilt cream and blood had caked hard on my dress and in my hair. I was stiff with bruises, reaction and pain and hardly able to walk. Afterwards it was not possible to work out why the accident happened. To my knowledge, my husband never had the van examined for a possible fault. Two days later, while I was in bed, my handbag was stolen from my dressing table, snatched through the low open window. The thief was so quick. Though I saw the unknown African, I could not move quickly enough, because of my injuries, to stop him. By the time my shouts alerted the family, he was long gone.

Directly after Christmas Grace went south for a break. During that time her British Passport was stolen. The real shock came when the British High Commission in Lusaka, who had issued it, refused to replace it. Born in Bulawayo, when Southern Rhodesia was a crown colony, she was registered British at birth and had held a British passport since she was 12 years old. Now in the changing political climate, neither her British registered birth certificate, nor British parents could help. It did not make sense, and was deeply shocking, but at the passport office, the authorities were adamant. Our appeals fell on deaf ears. We commenced proceedings to apply Zambian citizenship since Grace had lived in the territory continuously since she was three weeks old. Though we produced a complete dossier to verify this it was to prove futile.

There was a sequel to the church leaders' disquiet regarding Gordon's questionable behavior. The pastor, who still harbored grave doubts, came out to the farm, having told Gordon he wanted to talk us both. Gordon told me the pastor was coming, saying that the pastor had urgent, confidential church business to talk over with him, and I should leave them uninterrupted. On the day, Gordon met our pastor's car in the drive and took him directly down by the river. From the house, I could see the two men sitting and talking. After an hour or so, Gordon walked the pastor back up the far side of the lawn, to the drive where his car was parked out of my sight. I heard the car going up the drive. It did not pass the house. Later Gordon came back to the house without saying anything about the visit.

Years later, in Cape Town, when we were on a visit to that same pastor, I learned Gordon had actually told him I was away from home that day, so sure was he that I would do exactly as he said and not come to join them. I began to understand how much I had been manipulated. The pastor went away that day more or less convinced by his assurances, but still rather uneasy.

Cap, a friend of ours who had come to the end of his tour of duty on a particular mission station came to see Gordon. He said he had another year or so to go on his work permit and wondered whether he could be of use to us. Because he had three children at school in Lusaka he would need housing for his family. Since he had hopes that the work of Evangelical Outreach would resume Gordon agreed to let them live rent- free at the, then vacant farm manager's house. They came and were given a free allowance of produce and milk from the farm. I welcomed having them alongside, so sure that their input would be positive.

Shortly after this, in January, Stuart out with friends in my car was involved in an accident that severely damaged the car, though he was not hurt badly. Still not fully recovered from my own accident, I went down to Salisbury, Rhodesia/Zimbabwe in early February for a convalescent short break with friends. I came back feeling very much better. The only immediate concern on my mind was the fact that Gordon had not followed through and done what he should have, following our trip north.

Now, when I asked him what he intended doing in response to the advice he had been given, he made excuses, and rationalized, as to why he had not done so. When I attempted to encourage him to do this he became extremely angry. Again I glimpsed the provoking spirit that was prevailing in him, and which was diametrically opposed to the Spirit that was in me. He decided to go England and was away two months. This time my keen disappointment only served to underline my other growing anxieties. My health was deteriorating, and financial difficulties were increasing in the farm business.

Months went by and there was no progress in the matter of Grace's citizenship. Stuart, who was marking time before going to college in America, worked on the farm that season. His one desire was to fly and after much effort, he won a place at LeTourneau College in Texas that specialized in Engineering and Flight. In April he was welding security bars on one of our houses and thoughtlessly forgot to snap his visor down. In screaming agony I rushed him into town for treatment. He was blind for two weeks, in a great deal of pain. We did not know until the bandages came off, whether or not his sight had been permanently damaged. Thankfully his eyes were quite healthy.

Gordon returned and especially since I was feeling increasingly ill, I was relieved for him to take responsibility for the farm. A few weeks later Stuart suffered a bad motorbike accident. The year was becoming a nightmare.

The hospital had no plaster to immobilize Stuart shattered leg, so he lay packed in sandbags while we radioed to the nearest mission hospital, who kindly spared us some. Thankfully, we organized its transport up to Lusaka. Meanwhile, I grew weaker in body and the accumulated effects of recent events took its toll. I was fast becoming conditioned to expect more disasters, and the one I feared most was what was happening to Gordon and me. My doctor prescribed Lorexepam, trade name "Ativan." It was the ultimate snare that would bring me down.

Designed to allow a person to cope in a time of crisis, "Ativan" pills were small, blue and oblong. The assumption by the medical profession was that once the period of crisis was over, the patient would not need them. My prescription was one in the morning and one at night. I never took more than this. At first they helped me and I was coping so much better. A few weeks after they were prescribed, Stuart, now recovered, left for America.

That same week, I was so weak one day, I actually slid down the wall upon which I was leaning, onto the floor and could only crawl to my bedroom. A subsequent consultation with my doctor led to arrangements for me to have surgery in South Africa. My doctor renewed my prescription for "Ativan" to tide me over. In mid-September, Gordon drove me to Durban in Natal where arrangements were made for surgery two weeks later. Meanwhile, we stayed with a former neighbor who now lived at Margate, some 60 miles south of Durban. She also very kindly invited me to convalesce in her home.

Such was the economic state of Zambia at the time that we were officially not allowed to take any money out of the country. I was glad that our car was originally registered in South Africa otherwise we would have been required to deposit its worth at both Zambia and Zimbabwe borders. Unofficially, we had a tiny amount of U.S. and South African cash from friends to help.

In Durban we stayed in a missionary guesthouse the night before I entered the hospital. Gordon remained there a few days, though I know he found it restrictive. He actually met a stripper at this time, even bringing her to meet me. I did not know what she did at the time but, surprisingly she came to visit me in hospital and I was able to talk to her about Christ. She said she would come again so I obtained a Bible through a local church visitor and gave it to her. Years later, I met her unexpectedly. She had long since left that job, married, and testified that she had come to Christ.

After a few days Gordon decided to return to Zambia and went while I was still in the hospital. When I was discharged, a friend drove me to Margate on the coast where I remained to convalesce. But in a day or two I felt extremely ill again. The local doctor put me back on "Ativan". When I explained where I was from, he said he had become used to European women coming from the north fraying at the edges and dismissed me with a fatherly pat and wished me well.

Thankfully, all seemed well, but it was almost Christmas before I was strong enough to travel home. Through various agencies, and one particular friend in England, I was able to collect enough money together for the return airfare and a cash gift to my friend in Margate to cover the cost of my visit. The flight back to Lusaka was nerve racking. For some reason, our plane had to divert into Mozambique to refuel. There we sat without being allowed to leave our seats, for a couple of hours in sweltering heat with only a lot of soldiers and a dilapidated collection of army type huts to watch. It did not appear to be a regular civil airfield. However, we eventually touched down in Lusaka safely, but the plane was so late, people meeting the plane had been advised to go home. I was exhausted and this was the last straw. I did not have taxi-fare for the twenty-five mile long journey to the farm. Finally, in response to my telephone call, Gordon reappeared after what seemed like hours, and took me home.

There had been several disquieting indications of discord between the children and their father. How much was due to ordinary teen-age angst, I could not guess, nor did I understand the flashes of real animosity in their relationship. The knowledge that they had become aware of his infidelity with at least one Zambian woman came to me much later. It distressed me greatly whenever this hostility surfaced, but at the time I had no way of knowing its cause. My perception could not plumb its roots, and the truth proved to be far beyond my imagination.

Grace was still living in the city and working as a Legal Secretary. There was no progress on her citizenship application. I wanted to go to England to see my family in Solihull and to extend my convalescent period. But Gordon kept telling me I should not go in the winter, and it was March before he relented and bought me a ticket. During the flight over that night I felt feverish and unwell, but put it down to exhaustion. But no sooner had I arrived in my brother-in-law's house in Croydon, near London, on the first lap of my journey home I collapsed with an extremely high temperature.

Then it was an ambulance to the hospital and isolation. I had acute malaria.

Two weeks later, still shaky and feeling weak, I arrived in Solihull. I was so run down I developed a sinus abscess. Not long afterwards, my mother broke her hip. Her condition gave us all grave concern, for she had to wait days for a hospital bed. By the time I finally returned to Lusaka early in May, I was neither rested nor prepared for another crisis.

During my time in England, I had a few brief letters from Gordon, only written in general terms about the farm and so on, none really personal or with any specific news. But a lot had been going on. Apparently without me at home, certain inappropriate things about his behavior had come to the notice of the other people. Cap confronted him and was shocked to be rebuffed.

Meanwhile a missionary in Zimbabwe, who was aware of our work, but did not know us personally, had a dream one night. Convinced it was from God, he was impelled to travel nearly three hundred miles to the farm to bring God's warning to Gordon. He located the farm and made contact with Cap, whom he knew. Cap gathered a group of some four or five other godly, highly respected brethren from Lusaka. Together they faced Gordon with this warning and pleaded with him at length.

This confrontation took place the day after I returned from England, before I could come to grips with what was happening. I was not told of the warning until afterwards. After they arrived, the men ushered Gordon down to the empty 'Boathouse', only telling me they wished to be private and asked me to stay away. They did not explain why they were there.

When they emerged, several hours later, I was waiting on the patio. Gordon brushed by me into the house, and I asked Cap for an explanation. No doubt he was tired, but he just said, "I suggest you ask your husband that." None of the other brethren approached me. They were already on their way to their cars. I went into the house to talk to my husband.

Obviously whatever had taken place had left him very angry. Stubbornly he would not talk about it, neither could I glean anything much from Cap, though later he did tell advise me about the warning: that if my husband would not truly repent and be accountable, he was going to lose everything he held dear.

The following week brought me a letter from Zimbabwe in which the messenger said that after the confrontation the group were not convinced of his true repentance, though they pleaded with him with much prayer. Therefore they ended the day in warning him further. His show of remorse fell away, and this attitude gave them deep concern. They had finished up invoking the disciplinary scriptures as found in 1 Corinthians: Chapter 5, regarding sexual immorality. Verses 4 and 5 say, *"When you are assembled in the name of our Lord Jesus, and the power of our Lord Jesus is present, hand this man over to Satan, so that the sinful nature may be destroyed and his spirit saved on the day of the Lord."*

The writer warned me anything was possible now. I could expect anything to happen, anything at all, even my husband's death. He then went on to suggest that I could show the letter to Gordon if I wished.

The letter gave me a considerable jolt and I took it to Cap, who offered to come with me, if I decided to confront my husband with it, which I did. We sat down with Gordon in the study and I asked him to read it. His reaction dismayed me even more. He read it and tossed it contemptuously to one side. Badly upset, I grabbed my car keys and left the house. I drove blindly into town, and arrived abruptly in a friend's driveway in a flood of tears. I do not think I made any sort of sense to her or her husband, and they just let me weep. Hours later, they kindly escorted me back as far as the farm gate. But I was horrifically alarmed and could only think of getting away.

Shortly afterwards, this same friend told me she was driving down to Kariba, and I begged a lift. Not really thinking straight, I took my passport and what little money I could find. At the border, I hitched a lift across, and made my way to a hotel nearby where I took a room. The manager and his wife were Christians who were known to me. It was in my mind to ask for their help, but there was no opportunity that night. I wanted to find a lift south but not having adequate money I could not think what to do beyond that. I spent the first night mainly weeping in great distress, and I wrote a couple of letters to friends. Next morning, after I posted them, I realized they probably made little sense.

The following morning there was no opportunity to talk to the manager and his wife together because they were very busy. They said they would try and find time for me later. Before I could think what to do, Gordon showed up while I was at lunch in the dining room. With his usual outward show of urbane charm, he gripped my arm cruelly and walked me out the door. He escorted me back to my room and insisted I get my things together, then hustled me to his car. His whole manner was intimidating, and he drove the hundred miles or so to the farm in grim silence. I had neither the physical or emotional strength to resist. The Psalmist's words once again echoed in my mind *"Listen to my cry, for I am in desperate need, rescue me from those who pursue me, for they are too strong for me..."*

Not long after that, in a painful formal meeting, my husband was disciplined and put out of the very church he had helped establish. Pam, who also attended there, was severely censured.

Chapter 20
The Siege of Honor

My attempted defection had only made matters worse. It was difficult for me to carry on with any semblance of normality before other folk on the farm, particularly our new farm manager. Shortly afterwards, Gordon became severely ill with hepatitis. For several weeks he lay ill in bed and deteriorated to a skeleton covered with sagging yellow skin. Cap came down often to sit with him graciously offering to pray with him but Gordon would have none of it. I tried time and again to get him to talk, and assured him of my full support if he would attempt to face up to things, but he was adamant; he would not. I watched as he stiffened his neck and refused to bow before the Lord. Earlier that year, he had surprised me by appointing a new farm manager. What governed his choice was anyone's guess. She was a sophisticated, young redhead of acid wit and patronizing disposition. Forced to deal with her during his illness, she was a constant thorn in my flesh.

Once on his feet again, though it was a considerable time before he was strong, Gordon busied himself with the farm. His attitude toward Cap remained distant and hostile, but strangely he did not tell him to leave. But the seething anger remained and on one occasion, when Cap and his wife rendered me a service, his anger was loosed again in real fury and threats.

It may have been only a verbal threat but I felt torn apart and at the end of my tether. Later, I went up to Cap's house to talk to him, and asked him if he and his wife would pray with me about the situation that now existed, and the state of the farm business. Cap invited me to sit down but said he would not pray with me. Instead he took me to task for being passive. It was especially difficult as I had been fighting for so long and so welcomed Cap's input. I was thankful for his presence, and what I believed was a positive contribution.

If only Cap and his colleagues had briefed me fully and kept me in the picture, how much grief that would have saved. I always believed they were doing their best in a very difficult situation. But as it was, I was left guessing with imperfect understanding and bereft of support. Coming from the position of seemingly having done all the right things: I married for love, a Christian who gave every indication of being the real article and who persisted in claiming to be that in public, even to holding office in the church. I felt I had every right to expect him to adhere, or wish to adhere to that principle upon which we had based our mutual life. Surely clinging to that same standard and desiring above all things, his true repentance and the healing of our marriage was reasonable? But I was in the dark as to the true perverseness of his nature, and among the people round me, the last to learn the true extent of his perfidy.

When he went away, Gordon almost never set a date for his return. Because I did not know when to expect him, I often had to take the responsibility of making decisions if matters could not wait. His annoyance would rankle a long time, if those decisions did not please him.

My main reason for remaining now was Grace, trapped in Zambia without a passport. It had been two and half years and still we had no answer to her application for Zambian citizenship. The farm struggled financially and we were continuously plagued with robberies and stock theft. Periodically, I returned to my doctor in an effort to get help, but there was no help he could give me, save keep me on "Ativan" so I could keep going. Swamped by feelings of anxiety, palpitations and trembling became continuous. Back I would go to my doctor wondering whether these symptoms might be linked to the medication. I should have stopped taking the pills, but he did not suggest this. By this time, I seriously doubted my ability to function on my own away from familiar surroundings. I was trapped.

Then someone who had come to Christ on the farm paid us a brief visit. He stayed at Cap's house and, having somehow acquired knowledge of the most shameful thing of all, he came down to the farmhouse to see me.

Later, I learned that at the end of his first visit he became so troubled he had gone away to fast and pray. On his return, he too brought a word from God, warning Gordon that if he did not repent, God would bring upon him the thing he feared most, the loss of everything he held dear.

This young brother in Christ sat at my table over tea and without preamble expressed his outrage, that my husband had sexually abused our daughter.

"What I don't understand," he said, blazing with anger, "how you can just sit there. What are you doing?" The force of his rage totally overwhelmed me. I recoiled, stunned, stumbled to my feet and backed away from him in shock.

"My God, you didn't know, did you?" I heard the change in his voice as he reached out to me, but I was gone. Out of the door, across the lawn, only to fetch up hard against the barbed wire paddock fence. I stood there a long time, my hand absently brushing the protruding nails in the rough wood fence post. My mind grappled with this new horror as I tried to bring my sense of panic under control.

The truly awful thing was that I did not doubt him. Once the words had been said, they rang with a knell of fatal finality. I was only surprised by the realization that I was not surprised by this information. Shocked, angry, disgusted and heartbroken, but not surprised. It was as if the last piece of a jigsaw had slipped into place, and I could see at last the whole picture with its central flaw. This then was the rotten foundation stone that lay, unsuspected by me, beneath all we had endeavored to build. The lid was off the can of worms yet I had no way of knowing that day there was much more to come.

Overwhelmed with guilt that I had not known of this betrayal, I was dazed. How had I not known? How was it possible? Yet even while I shuddered in my soul, I knew it to be the truth for it explained so much that had eluded me. And why, dear God why had no one ever told me? Was this what people around me had known about, thought I condoned? Did they think I could possibly have been party to this betrayal of my children, this travesty of fatherhood? When I later learned just who had known, people I had worked with, those I called my friends, my anger, humiliation and despair were compounded. And later when I learned who else had been involved, my sense of devastation was overwhelming. I was totally gutted.

Later in private, I tried to find some gesture to express my deep anger, repugnance and grief. I wrenched my wedding ring off and threw it in the garbage bin. Then collapsed on the floor in a paroxysm of weeping which left me sick for days.

The screws were being tightened down on the coffin of my marriage. This knowledge was to change my life. It was the finishing stroke.

Whatever this young man said when he faced my husband and delivered his warning, neither spoke of it to me. He left immediately afterwards and returned to South Africa. Gordon suddenly announced he was going to America to visit Stuart and would then go on to England. In a few days he was gone. His parting words were that Cap and family had to be gone by the time he returned.

Cap did not have to be told. His work-permit was almost expired and they prepared to leave. They did not have enough money to ship their heavy goods so he came to me to ask for it. There was no problem about eventual repayment, and I was happy to help but at the time it was a strain on the farm finances. When the debt was settled very soon after, my husband stubbornly refused to pay it into the bank. It seemed he would rather nurse his anger. He never forgave me for this and other assistance I had given this family.

From time to time I felt overwhelmed by all that had happened and would sit shivering, my arms wrapped around my body, hugging myself as I wept for my children that by now were grown and away from home. Unable to form words to pray, I could only manage low, keening noises of anguish. Then panic attacks were added to my list of physical miseries. In desperation, I decided to go to England and consult my mother's doctor who I knew to be a Christian. When the time came to pay for my flight, in an agony of tension I had to borrow money from a friend. Only a week after Gordon returned, I left. I was in no state to confront him again. Also I was increasingly fearful of contracting AIDS or some other dread disease as a result of his careless immoral living. In short, I was in full flight.

The long weeks I spent in England in the autumn of 1984 were a seesaw of emotion. No doubt my family were distressed and puzzled to see me so distraught. I tried to explain but did not do very well. My mother's doctor was kind but unable to help. I was still only taking two tablets in 24 hours, but even before I got to England, I was trying to cut down by halving the tablets. But the resultant agitation and faintness made me even less able to function. We tried other medication, but I felt so ill, and became frightened of collapsing in public. So it was decided I should stay on the "Ativan." He had no other advice to offer at that time.

The spiritual highlight of this time in England was being invited for a weekend's fellowship with friends of my mother's doctor. The Lord met me in a wonderful way and there I found the first powerful ministry into my need. Despite the fact I had not solved my problem with "Ativan" and was far from stable, physically and emotionally, I nevertheless, received new insight and strength as I listened to God's Word. Again the conviction that He would help me rise up had encouraged me.

Perhaps my judgment was at fault, but I decided to go back. I did not want to, but with my experience with emergencies and political instability there was no way I would permanently leave Zambia while Grace remained there without a passport unable to leave. She was living in town and rarely came home. The rift between her father and herself was complete. Right on the heels of my return, she saw a window of opportunity and successfully applied for a one-off travel document to go to Zimbabwe. I went with her, and in two days she obtained a Zimbabwe birth certificate, identity card and applied for a passport. Thirty days later, we were advised her passport was ready and I flew down to collect it. We had gone through too much to risk it in the post. She had been stateless for two years and ten months. In possession of a new passport, Grace set about raising her airfare to England. She was determined to leave Africa, the land of her birth, for good.

Grace left early in February. Shortly afterwards Gordon decided to visit our former pastor in Cape Town. He said he needed counsel and help. I wanted to believe him and hoped our friend would indeed help. Within a couple of days he left, but once again set no return date. Almost immediately I was faced with a crisis in Stuart's affairs.

For along time, Zambia had been in such economic straits that no foreign exchange was allowed, save for further education. And now the restrictions made getting money out of Zambia well nigh impossible. Also Gordon had left me when the farm business was showing unmistakable signs of something amiss. Time and again, I was reminded of God's warning given to Gordon. Now Stuart was suffering, having to give up halfway through his training in his chosen profession. After an agonizing interval, he changed his chosen career in flight to one of business. Meanwhile, he worked a forty-hour week, in the city's ambulance service, for nearly another three years to pay his own way.

This time, with my husband away, I really was not fit to carry on alone. The farm was a heavy burden. Though I was thankful Grace had got out, I had no idea when I would see her again. I missed her.

Moving in a deepening cloud of despondency and fear, for which I later learned the "Ativan" was largely responsible, I struggled on from day to day. I felt increasingly hopeless and helpless. Because my doctor seemed incapable of understanding or of offering some solution, I was on a treadmill of misery.

There was no one around, except the Zambian staff and a former school friend of our boys, working as a driver. Gordon had made no indication when he was likely to be back, neither did he write or telephone. In March I had a visitor. We had a mutual friend in England, and this lady had written asking if she could break her journey to Zimbabwe in order to meet me. I had agreed and she duly arrived in Lusaka and her company for a few days was welcome.

By this time, I was experiencing several symptoms of long term "Ativan" dependency and felt ill all the time. Sharing my fears with this lady, led us both to make it a particular matter for prayer and I became convinced that somehow, I had to help myself, if ever I was to win free.

My visitor went on her way and I was alone except for Salu my house servant. He came to work for us almost twenty years before this date, first as a gardener. After some years, I brought him into the house and taught him to clean and launder. He was a very quiet African with a gentle, ready smile whose personality suited me. Over the years we had established a bond. We had sat together on my back doorstep holding each other in grief when his twin daughters died; now he hovered and brought me a tea tray from time to time, as I lay by the hour ill and frightened.

I had come to the end of the road. There was no help but what I could muster for myself with the help of God. I had become convinced my life was effectively finished unless I could regain control. That evening I decided I would never take another "Ativan" tablet and I did not. I shut myself in my absent daughter's bedroom and lay on the floor, in total reliance upon God. All I could think of was Esther's prayer, "if I perish, I perish." Hours later, I dragged myself onto the bed and lay there with my heart pounding.

Chapter 21
Green Apple Soap

I felt extremely ill and weak the following day. I was so frightened at being alone on the farm, I telephone Mrs. Mac to ask if I could come in to town to stay with her, but she already had Mac's boss there, so I asked the farm driver to get me to another acquaintance's house. They took me in but warned me they had plans for the weekend and would be away a lot. None of us had any idea how ill I was and they continued to come and go all that weekend. A long time afterwards I wondered why they had not summoned medical help for me. But that thought joined the litterbin of unanswered questions collected throughout this period. Alone in the spare room I struggled with a truly vicious headache and by that evening I was hypersensitive to light and sound. Unable to stand properly, I became delirious.

The walls alternately leaned over me or receded, changing into distorted shapes. I had lots of other visual disturbances as I struggled through another day. At times I was aware that I was talking, knowing I made no sense, the babble of words echoing in the empty house. In other, more lucid moments, I repeated God's promise to get me through this terrible time.

Strangely, I awoke next morning feeling better with a clearer head. It was Sunday and I felt even better after a bath and shampoo. As I made my way down the hall from the bathroom, my host met me and asked if I would like to go to Church. Striving for some semblance of normality, I thanked him and said 'yes'. He and his partner did not appear to notice anything strange about me, nor did they make any comment about me not being well over the preceding 48 hours.

By the time we were due to leave the house, I felt rather odd again. I had taken a little breakfast, after eating almost nothing in the two days beforehand and I felt very weak. Again I began to feel disorientated. As I approached the car, it changed shape and it was difficult for me to remain steady and my vision became blurred. Strangely, my hosts made no comment and did not seem to be aware of any of this.

This did not puzzle me at the time because I was so taken up with feeling weird and trying to act normally. I don't think I succeeded which, in retrospect is even stranger. They dropped me off at the church entrance and drove off. Up to that point I had assumed they were coming to the church as well, as they sometimes did. I remember going towards someone I knew and reaching out as I greeted her and remarked on her child's very pretty new dress. She grabbed the child in a very defensive manner and backed away from me.

The church was full and yet I felt curiously as if in a cocoon but when the faces began to distort and the sounds echoed and surged, coming at me in waves, I could not understand any of it. The next thing I was being helped out into a side room and later taken to the house of an acquaintance, where I lay almost round the clock till the next morning when I was taken to hospital. Strangely though there were lucid gaps in the day and I kept a fair reckoning of the time through the night. Just before sunrise I got up off the bed and found my bible was laying on the dressing table. In it I wrote a note, dated it and had a precious time of lucid prayer while the house lay sleeping around me.

My recollection of visiting my doctor's office was extremely patchy but I remember clearly who was in the ambulance with me. I will always remember her kindness to me that day.

I awoke to see my hand stretched out against a roughly painted wall. Above my head was a frieze of bright flowers. As I turned over I became conscious that I was just lying on top of a high iron bedstead. I gazed silently at the faces that swam around me above carelessly arranged cotton wraps or shifts. No one spoke. The patients, all African women, were staring at me curiously. I was in a locked ward at Chainama, Lusaka's mental hospital.

The room held six beds. The wall opposite had holes in it and a protruding pipe where a washbasin had been taken away and not replaced. Necessity helped me push off the bed and investigate the toilet in the corner. There was urine on the floor, the cracked basin held an unsavory residue because it did not flush properly. There was no paper and no door.

I kept telling the nurse and the doctor when he came, about leaving off the "Ativan" suddenly. It was impossible to know if they believed me as no one commented on this or questioned me about it. The most disconcerting thing was that no one talked with me. After the doctor's visit, I was taken for a shower in an open communal shower room. It was while I was standing in line, and naked, waiting to be handed a course cotton overall, that Pam came up to me. She worked in this hospital.

At a time when she was endeavoring to get her life together, before I knew the full extent of her relationship with my husband, I had bought her uniforms in England, as a gift. For a moment our meeting seemed so unreal. There she stood, so crisp and confident, and though she appeared sincere, I did not trust her. I was only conscious of my total humiliation.

But, at least I felt clean now, but the day was not over. My mind was clear and I was lying on top of my bed trying to make sense of what was happening. Gordon walked in with a couple of hospital staff. He may have been shocked to suddenly return and find me there, but to me he was not real. It was as if a pane of glass separated us. He went away again. My greatest blessing was my friends Mrs. Mac and the doctor who had been so kind after the raid. Mrs. Mac brought me the gift of some Green Apple soap. The next day I was moved into a small open ward, and although it had two beds, I was on my own.

The clean, cool smell of that soap became my focus. Its evocative fragrance reminded me of all that was good and clean, pure and unsullied. I held it to my face when I prayed and thanked God for I every time I washed.

Although staggering a bit on "jelly-legs" and at times a bit disorientated, I was in the rehabilitation block and able to freely walk around. At first, I had no other toilet things and no underwear, but one of my first visitors took a message and the pastor's wife sent me in some of hers. The smallest thing now became a blessing. In the communal ablution block, attached to the rehabilitation ward where I now resided, out of eight toilets, only one had a door. It was always available when I needed a little privacy.

Then Gordon came again. He sat and talked to me, even showed me photos of his time in South Africa. I still did not really think of him as being actually there. In many ways, I was fast returning to normality but this one fixation remained. He continued to be more of a ghost figure.

Meanwhile, I had a room of my own and even some books to read, kindly sent by my doctor friend. Mrs. Mac was particularly kind and came in regularly. She also sent in food to relieve the basic Zambian diet of *nshima* and relish. I walked among the flowerbeds and began to feel strong again. Another friend arrived in tears and brought a truly gorgeous armful of flowers. So I had privacy and beauty and my perfumed soap. I walked for hours in the grounds and beyond, around the field at the back. That was my prayer place, where, day- by- day, I claimed my life back.

Although by now I had some clothes from home, and was feeling so much better, in one aspect I was trapped. Still, I clung to the conviction that Gordon was dead. So real was this in me that no matter how much other people told it was untrue, I did not believe them. On one memorable very hot day, even with my doctor present, I would not even take a glass of cold water from him, even though I was thirsty. No doubt all this was a shock for Gordon. Apparently, he had not wanted to come and see me straight away after his return, but delayed. Would what was happening to me have enough impact to bring him to accept a degree of accountability and want to face up to it? Even to those nearest to him, it was difficult to tell, but as it happened he did talk to a Zambian Pastor when they met in town, and he came to see me.

When this Christian friend came into my room, he sat down and simply told me I'd got it wrong. Gordon was indeed alive. I just stared at him. What reason would I have not to believe him? I trusted him. He would not lie to me. In a moment, it all came right side up, and I was mortified that I could have done such a thing. I sent him off to tell Gordon to come again as soon as possible then flew around to the nurses' office to tell them what had happened. Less than forty -eight hours later I was home. In all, it had been ten extraordinary days.

However I was not able to rest. Gordon announced his intention of taking me and returning to South Africa later that same weekend. He had informed my doctor of this. When I was released, he was given the letter to take with us regarding my medication, which was designed to carry me through the next period of recovery. However, before we could fly, he spent a busy day tying up farm business and leaving instructions. Because of his previous absence, I was coerced into dealing with letters, farm business etc., and spent some hours in the office.

Strangely, this was not difficult at this stage of my recovery. With typical pharisaic absorption, my husband made no allowances for what I had so recently been through. Nevertheless, except for a slight headache from the intensity of concentration I needed to focus on the task, I managed very well. Then he took me off to Cape Town.

It was all ostensibly for my convalescence, but once in Cape Town, he revealed plans to stay there. It was not that easy. One could not work without having residential status and one could not become a resident quickly without work. When my tablets were finished we went to a local doctor and the prescription was refilled. Whatever happened to the letter regarding a gradual phasing down of the medication I do not know. I was not that well. The new medication brought on lack of concentration to the point where I could not read or watch TV. The days dragged. A former Lusaka friend, now living in the Cape, lent us a car once or twice a week. It was wonderful to be able to drive round the countryside, but then it became obvious he was looking for work.

My lack of concentration was very difficult. I had difficulty in sitting for long and church services were an agony, as was being in a crowd. Gordon walked me around a lot, but I began to have an unreal sense of distance and was afraid of public places. The space around me became distorted. He began to go out and about without me, often late in evening. Then a young friend of his came down to stay nearby and the two men went off. Sometimes they went for whole days, to climb Table Mountain and other activities. Our guestroom had a well- stocked bookcase, but I could not read at all, whereas formerly, I was always a keen reader.

It was on one of these days I was alone, that the young couple, assisting the pastor, invited me to go to lunch with them. Gratefully grasping at this chance not to be alone, I went to the front door. As I put my foot out from the step, a huge chasm opened up in front of me and I recoiled. They could not get me to cross the drive to the car. I was the victim of agoraphobia.

Strangely, Gordon did not seem to notice. But did he? I could not go out without holding on him. If he walked a little ahead, I was terrified he would disappear. He accepted an invitation to go up to George, a lively little town along the coast for a few days. It was difficult for me. One day our friends took us for a picnic on the beach. Every time our hostess and her husband walked away from us, they seemed to disappear off the edge of the horizon. I clung to my husband's side. It was at George that I was first aware that that I sometimes drooled. Once again I was moving in unstable surroundings. Our hosts were kindness itself, but busy, articulate people. It was difficult for me to sustain a conversation, watch TV or read, indeed I could not concentrate on anything.

We went out one day in the car miles into the country where Gordon said he was trying to get a job. It was a pig farm. Set in most beautiful, rolling countryside, it nevertheless had no other farm or house in sight. The house was dark and dreary and I suddenly had a picture of what my life would be if ever I got trapped here. I began to fight back.

The next time Gordon went off for a day, I took some money from the drawer in the bedroom and forced myself to go out. I was really frightened, but more scared of the alternative. The household had got used to us being independent, Gordon out a great deal, me 'resting in my room'. So no one took any notice as I crept out. I had to cling to every available thing I could see to get from the house down the short drive to the street. I felt I was trying to make my way blindfolded, so hesitant were my steps. I made the street, and, taking a deep breath, I turned towards the shops, keeping touch with the garden walls and hedges as I went. Getting myself into a shop was a major effort, but I made it, and trembling, managed to buy some pins, a pattern and some wool. Still shaking and feeling very strange but heartened, I slowly and painstakingly started home. Still touching walls, bushes and gateposts as I went, I was still fighting a feeling of being drawn off the pavement, but I reached the house again - exhausted but safe.

Others were living in our house and managing our farm. I learned that

Gordon had led them to believe we were not coming back. While I painfully tried to knit, I prayed using what I could remember of Hebrews Chapter 11 as a litany. *"By faith Abel..., by faith Noah...,by faith Abraham...,"* by faith I was going to get out of this hideous situation. It did not matter how many mistakes I was making, striving to co-ordinate my shaky hands, the knitting became a focus for my will to endure.

Our host invited me to join him and two of his friends in their weekly game of Scrabble. I played very badly, even simple words were a struggle, but I was grateful to be taken out of the house. It was on one of these drives to his friends' house, that we talked and I discovered the truth about the incident of his visit to our farm long ago. He had been our pastor in Lusaka then, and had come out to the farm on that occasion, expressly to talk to us both. He spoke of his puzzlement and unease as Gordon had circumvented his opportunity to do so. Now he heard my side of that.

It was to be a long time before I fully realized what a dangerous thing I had done in taking myself off "Ativan" so abruptly. A considerable time would pass before I was privy to the information exposed by the media in England and the outpouring of information that would then be available on this and other tranquilizers.

I began to nag Gordon about going back to Lusaka. His plans to find work and apply to reside in South Africa were not working out. I kept on talking about going back and became more insistent. Finally, he agreed that we should go.

Chapter 22
The Shining Night

We came home from Cape Town via Johannesburg. There we stayed overnight with the friends who had lent us their house after the raid. It was difficult for me. Struggling with the irrational fear that something would prevent me from reaching home, I was ill at ease and still slightly off balance. Most worrying of all, I knew I was losing control of my facial muscles and the knowledge made me feel clumsy and self-conscious.

When we arrived home safely I was filled with relief and thankfulness. But even the jolt of having to go into one of the guest rooms could not distract me from my most urgent need, to reach medical help.

Insistent that I get to the hospital early the next day to find the doctor who had prescribed for me, I was given the first appointment after lunch. As we sat outside his office waiting for him to return from lunch, I saw him approach down the hall. Even as he came up to me, he was searching my face. He gave an exclamation of dismay and abruptly said he wanted to speak to my husband first. Did he query what had happened to his letter of instruction regarding the management of my medication? I never knew. But I did get a strong impression that I had reached him none too soon. He put me on a short course of something else to steady things, and to my relief it worked. I soon felt better and my slack facial muscles improved to near normal. Within a few weeks I was totally off medication altogether.

Within a few days of our return, new arrangements were made and we were back in the farmhouse. Things were much the same, but not the same as before. Changes had been made to the house but I did not really care. Other than look after domestic details I had no role to play. No body came and in many respects it was a strange time. The farm was gradually but surely diminishing and I was in the odd position of observer only.

Outwardly the farm was functioning but my awareness of God's warning sharpened my perception. Our specialist poultry-raising unit was failing because there seemed to be no market. There was a definite air of dejection among the staff. Gordon switched to table poultry but we were not equipped for that and it was a disaster because we had no adequate refrigeration facility. The plethora of wasted, rotting birds brought a plague of flies.

Finally he gave that up. The garden produce dwindled away. On the top field where I had often grown a commercial crop of Sweet Peas for the city florists, the cane frames lay discarded in untidy heaps. The staff began to go.

Chabaila and Salu, those long serving stalwarts, still carried on. It was a relief to have Salu's help in the house for although there was not so much to do, I was still far from strong. Because there was no other work for him, Chabaila was put to work making new pews for a church in town.

In the meantime, Gordon decided to take me to Kenya for a short holiday. Once airborne, I was visited again by the odd fear of flying just as I was in South Africa recently. This period was the only time in my life that this happened. When the Captain said a few words to the passengers and jocularly mentioned what our height was off the ground, I nearly blacked out and could not bear to look at the windows for the rest of the journey.

It was never really clear why we should go to Kenya just then after being away for so long but recently. Perhaps the ambivalent atmosphere or a sense of being unable to reverse the downward trend on the farm governed my husband's decision. Though I felt as though I was merely tagging along, I tried to enjoy the loveliness of Amboseli Game Park and Lake Nyivasha's spectacle of teeming thousands of flamingos. But the fleeting presence of odd moments of feeling unreal within my body kept me from relaxing completely.

Not long after we returned to the farm, I was offered a chance to go England with people I trusted but I knew that if I did I would never return. I was not fit enough to manage on my own. Gordon had long since removed my signature from our bank account and I had no other money. Though I would be welcome in my brother's home, I could not contemplate that in my condition for although it would suit for a short time I had no idea how long it would be before I could really get on my feet. They were loving and generous but had no spare room. A temporary stay was possible, but when would I gain the energy to move out to forge a new life? In the event it was no go. Gordon refused to pay my fare so I remained. I could only pray the words from Psalm 143, "...*For your name's sake O Lord, preserve my life; in your righteousness, bring me out of trouble.*"

The days dragged on and the farm ticked over uneasily. I witnessed the slow but steady breakdown of everything around me. Ever mindful of God's warning, I watched as first one thing, then another fell apart. Once reasonably well off, we became poor, plagued by stock theft, break-ins at the farmhouse and other buildings. Then another vehicle was stolen. Tools and equipment evaporated. Finally, for the first time, disease struck our stock.

Gordon had a sailboat of which he was inordinately proud though he refused to use lifejackets, which was distressing to me when he took the children out. Once the boat capsized on the Kafue River and we narrowly missed total tragedy. He took the boat to Lake Iteshi-Teshi and there it sank in a freak storm. When he finally got it raised and back home, he could not get the material to mend it. It was never fixed. For years he had a small piece of land at the lakeside where he wanted to build a little holiday fishing camp. It was never finished. Finally, the half-built foundation became an eyesore to the neighboring plot owners and they complained. He was forced to let it go.

It was difficult for me to have so little to do but wait for my situation to change. I felt detached from the problems that arose. Gordon had spells of apathy but did not welcome any input from me. Everyone was going through the motions but the heart had gone from it. Freed from the "Ativan" addiction I held on to the promises God had given me. I waited.

With no outside role, I focused within. It was a period of deep heart searching and prayer. I dwelt in the psalms where I could identify with so many of God's people who had striven and agonized, suffered and ultimately triumphed with joy. They expressed so much of such experiences and many passages seemed to speak into my situation so well. I wanted above all, to find my own balance in what was unfolding. I sought my own truth anxious only not to miss the Holy Spirit's leading. *If I say "Surely the darkness will hide me and the light become night around me, even the darkness will not be dark to you, the night will shine like the day, for darkness is as a light to you." Psalm 139: v 11 and 12.*

There were no guests now. The guesthouses only held dust and spiders. To what extent the wider Christian circle knew of our private lives, I was not sure. But one day, friends who had once been influenced towards Christ in our home, called in and in my own sitting room, said to me: "We thought you must condone your husband's behavior. You are still here, are you not?" The hurt went very deep. Associated shame made me silent. My credibility was gone, my witness compromised and in the complexity of the situation, I had no defense.

Winter came again. There were no crops in the fields and almost no staff left. We were alone in a silent house with very little to say to each other. Suddenly Gordon decided we should go to England and my heart leapt in thankfulness. It had been a most difficult year. Every time a new blow had fallen, I had gone to the Lord in anguish about my own life going down the drain. He had restored the core of inner peace within me and helped me wait patiently. Now the door was beginning to open.

The cattle were the last liquid- Asset. Foreign Exchange would now let us take a small travel allowance out of the country. Without the sale of the cattle we could not do this or pay for our air tickets. At last the time came when the cattle were re-located and tickets were booked for August 27th

1986. I gradually began my farewell to all I had loved in this place. Only I knew I would never come back.

I walked in the morning sun beneath the towering eucalyptus trees that lined the farm drive and, remembering the rainy day when we had planted them more than twenty five years before, I touched their fragrant leaves. Looking up to watch their stately movement against the sky, I thought about my early hopes and their slow demise.

Crossing the fallow fields, I came to the paddock flanked by empty poultry pens. The field was empty now. My boxer dog always had an affinity with the two bullocks that grazed there. Their job had been to draw the farm cart and she would play around them or sit beside them for hours. I remembered how her chestnut head would bob up above the long grass when she heard the cart's approach and how she would prance in the sunlight in playful invitation.

The dark sweeping cassia trees now only shaded the deserted truck camping ground and, at the end of the avenue, Sharon Cottage stood vacant. There was no sound of singing wafted by the breeze from across the river, no sound of a tractor in the fields.

One somnolent afternoon, I sat sorting various papers on my desk for the last time. The wide windows were open and I looked down across the lawns to the silent, shuttered "Boathouse". I heard the sharp 'clunk' of Salu's axe as he gathered firewood and a wood dove's evocative call from the wild fig tree beyond the dairy.

The river rushed over the waterfall heedless of the loss of children's laughter. I walked the path alongside its cool depths and passed by the farm manager's house, now let to strangers. Crossing the cattle drift, I took the sloping path to the Evangelical Outreach campsite. I let myself remember the fun and sense of achievement of the early days. Now the damaged houses stood silent, showing all too clearly their scars. In the long grass I stumbled over the last termite riddled remains of a few roof timbers that had been intended for the new hall. I stood on the veranda of the first house we had built at the campsite, looking down towards the river, remembering the baptisms there, and prayed again that in God's grace something would endure.

For a brief moment I felt again the sting of a fleeting memory, my piercing disappointment at Gordon's chauvinistic refusal to allow me to be one of the trustees of "Evangelical Outreach". But like so much else, I had brought this hurt to the feet of Jesus and left it there, not wanting bitterness to mar my life further. So I said 'goodbye' to my ghosts and came away.

On the last evening I sat on the patio and watched the sun sink behind the trees on the riverbank. A goshawk launched from high up in the nande flame tree and skimmed the lawn in the brief dusk. His high, thin cry was a mournful echo to my own sad spirit. This was not my place anymore.

The following day I said farewell to Salu and walked out of my house. Chabaila stood respectfully on the patio, his gentle face compassionate and understanding as we shook hands. I think he knew we would not meet again and why. As the car drove away from the house, I did not look back. We drove past the derelict boat still lying under its shabby old canvas cover covered in dead leaves. The car swept up the drive and out to the main road. Gordon had told me right at the last that he still had things to do and would follow. I was to go alone and he would let me know when he could come. It was symbolic of our lives that would henceforth be apart.

Emotionless, we parted after I checked in at the airport. I sat in the departure lounge, my tired thoughts still drifting around what I was leaving. I believe Chabaila and Salu had come to Christ in those years, and many others. What was sound and lasting of any spiritual harvest was by the grace of God and only time and heaven would reveal its true worth. My critics had accused me of being passive, judging our work as worthless. My friends had simply melted away. Though I truly had not known of the canker that had destroyed us from within, I was now embarked on a journey of repentance and humble self-appraisal. I was not to know then that in God's grace, the Campsite would evolve and live again and that Yieldingtree would revive someday to beauty and even greater productivity and that my yet unborn granddaughters would play on its sunny lawns.

When my plane lifted off I looked down at the beloved land as it passed beneath me. I remembered how I had come to this rich, beautiful country in the early summer of my life, and now in its autumn I was leaving it, eroded and dry with poverty, riddled with AIDS and torn apart with war.

Chapter 23
Backlash

My daughter was at London Gatwick to meet me. As her arms went round me my tired spirit revived. I knew deep inside me that this was only the beginning of another phase. There were still so many lessons to be learned in compassion and forgiveness. We were survivors in the hands of a loving God and although we cannot know the length of it, grieving is for a season only. Even when sorrow remains there is hope in God's all redeeming love.

We had been offered the use of a cottage for a few months and it was good to feel we had a starting point. I knew myself to have little stamina and I needed time to decide what I would do. The cottage belonged to a friend of Gordon in Lusaka and was situated in a small village in Wiltshire. It was available from the beginning of October. In the meantime, I went to stay with Grace in Croydon.

On the first Sunday in her church, a stranger sitting at the back got to her feet and brought a prophetic message in the Spirit. As soon as she started to speak I felt it was for me. Grace felt the same and later, when I was introduced around after the meeting, the speaker also confirmed it, saying she recognized it as such as she met me face to face. She had said: "My daughter, I know the year you have lived through. Do not fear what is ahead. The problems of the past will not be repeated. You are landed on the solid rock."

The language and message was so similar to that which I had received in 1984. It was startling but encouraging and I took heart. Gordon sent word he would arrive by the end of September, and when he did, we went down to Wiltshire. God was very good to us. A friend from earlier days in Lusaka, who had been on vacation in Europe, arranged for us to take over his car. Although I was now on no medication whatsoever and generally feeling a great deal better, I was unsure what to do. I needed to be more settled within myself before I made any life changing decision.

It had only been possible to bring a small amount of money out of Zambia. We had to find some means of support in England, having no money there or pensions. Gordon was a fair amateur photographer and thought he could perhaps earn some money with it. So he decided on a photographic course. With winter coming on we settled into a rural life of walks, the occasional visit to a country event and long evenings by the fire. But he was uncommunicative and I was merely waiting.

He was soon restless and went off on various quests and outings connected to the photographic course. We were welcomed into an interdenominational group in another village. We made some plans for Christmas. Grace was coming down to stay for a few days and Stuart was coming from America for the holidays.

As the days shortened, Gordon toyed with other ideas of how to make a living in England. I knew the time was approaching when I must make a major decision, but while he was undecided, I was content for the moment. I endeavored to be quiet within myself, wanting to feel physically stronger. I knew I needed a little more time, to find the inner strength and opportunity to achieve my escape without risk of failure. I was looking forward to having my family around me for a while and busied myself with preparations for Christmas.

We had left the farmhouse just as it stood, not packed up, and before leaving, Gordon told me he had arranged for it to be let to a friend who wanted to move out of town. We had packed two tea chests only, all we were allowed to take out of Zambia. In one, I had put necessities to help us in England since there would be no money to set up a home to begin with, sheets, towels, a small amount of cutlery and dishes and the like. Gordon had prevailed in his choice to take books. On the flight I carried only a picture painted by Grace in addition to my suitcases. Neither of us had any winter clothes, but managed minimally to set ourselves up from the local charity shops.

In the mist of my quickening anticipation of the coming visits I was brought back to an urgent review of my situation with a jolt. With Gordon away for a day, I accidentally came across indisputable evidence he was again conducting an illicit sexual affair. I fought off waves of nausea, forcibly reminded again that there would be no peace in my life until I took action. My attempt to talk to him after his return failed. Every effort I made to confront him on the issues between us failed. He sensed at the onset what I was about and responded in anger or elusively slipped away. He disappeared for a few hours or a whole day. I had no one to talk to in that place and telephoned a pastor friend who had returned from Africa to settle not far away. He often visited a relation even nearer us to us, so he promised to come over and see me next time his wife and he were nearby. It happened on a day Gordon was away again and there was time to talk. It helped me a little, but of course, no one else could 'do' anything. It was all up to me.

Our two small boxes arrived. Because Gordon had not paid for the airfreight of these before leaving Lusaka, they had stood, obviously outside, until the new tenant of our house had taken the money to pay. The box of books was ruined with water, while my box of household necessities was damp at the bottom but unspoiled.

Christmas started out well, and it was a joy to see the children, grown as they were, Grace a legal secretary with a prestigious firm in the center of London, Stuart full of his college experiences in America. I tried to set my personal concerns aside but there were deep undercurrents. It was all too easy for a chance remark to cause hurt, no doubt stemming from bad memories. After the holiday, I waved my brother's car off and walked back into cottage. I found Gordon incensed that none of the rest of us wanted to spend a day of our precious time together, visiting an acquaintance of his, whom I had only met once and the others knew not at all. He was mad because typically, he had made arrangements without consulting us and would lose face pulling out.

Stuart and Grace left together, and the winter closed in. A blizzard hit us in the New Year and movement was restricted to chopping and hauling in wood to feed the big stone fireplace. The village was too small to have a shop and the necessary grocery shopping was a hazardous adventure in the narrow hilly lanes to the next village. Though it was only a day or two before we gained access to the main road while the countryside lay under a solid coat of snow, deep enough to alter the landscape. We took a few short exhilarating walks in heavy boots, muffled to the eyebrows, but between ourselves the tension remained.

Towards the end of January, I succumbed to a bad throat infection that left me feeling as though I was trapped in a time warp, drained and apathetic - I knew I must do something to change my circumstances, but felt temporarily powerless to engage in the battle again. Time and again, my mind rehashed what had happened. Had I been that naïve, that passive, that stupid? My mind turned in an endless spiral. I was aware that Cap's attitude at times had left me with scars because I had been so vulnerable. Nevertheless, I knew in my heart he had done his best in most trying circumstances, and I was grateful. We had parted well. Perhaps I was needlessly beating myself over the head about it all, but I still struggled to understand. What had kept me tied in that situation so long, especially those last few years? Still stateless without a passport Grace was the string; my long awaited hope for my husband; my belief in God's faithfulness, and my commitment. I could not regret my choices.

I drifted through a few more weeks, and suddenly it was Easter and Grace came down for the weekend. She sensed I hardly knew what to do, or where to go. She urged me to move out. I tried not to worry her with the knowledge that a couple of distressing symptoms that now bothered me for which I had no explanation. From time to time, I experienced a real lump in my throat and could not swallow or breathe properly. Though I tried to make light of it, she must have read in my face something of what that long, drawn out winter of tension and indecision had cost me.

That winter, as the snow had drifted across the monochrome landscape and made us prisoners of the cottage, I had tried hard to whip my flagging will to action. But I was penniless and homeless.

Deep down, I knew I had to get away, or the whole of the rest of my life was ruined. The sense of failure was profound. I felt I was losing myself, as the person I was and feared would never be again.

Easter was early and the weather glorious. Shortly afterwards we went to church in Salisbury one Sunday morning, before driving to Bath to visit my mother-in-law. Suddenly, some time into the service, I was riveted to hear the minister giving a warning in his sermon, the words almost identical to those warnings Gordon had received in Zambia. I looked sideways at Gordon reaching out to touch him, but his face was fiercely set, rigid with such stony anger, I felt chilled and looked away hurriedly. My eyes alighted on a banner, lit with a shaft of sunshine before me. Its text, surrounded by bright spring flowers, read:

"You will go out in joy and be led forth in peace; the mountains and the hills will burst into song before you, and all the trees of the field will clap their hands." Isaiah 55:12

Returning to our car after the service, he looked a little more approachable, I resolved to make one last attempt to get him to focus on what was between us. But as soon as I started to talk, he adroitly sidestepped the issue. "Talk? Why do you want to talk about us? Why should we?" He smoothly dismissed my attempts with a smile and once again I was reduced to ineffectual shadowboxing with words. In no way would he allow me to get near, so we lapsed into silence. At his suggestion we broke our journey to visit Wells Cathedral, which I had never seen, and while there, I became aware of an extraordinary phenomenon. It seemed as though a thick cloud had rolled between us like an encroaching fog. It was so real I looked around to see if other people around us were affected. But no, it seemed not, though the dark cloud looked real and almost solid to me. A weight descended on my spirit and lay upon my shoulders. We left the Cathedral and walked for a while in the sunshine, and the weight and the shadow remained. Inside I was weeping as the burden of grief I had held at bay for so long, struggled for expression as the last glimmer of hope died.

Outwardly, we resumed our journey and went through the motions of visiting, taking tea and driving home. I gazed unseeing at the passing scenery in the twilight. And again I was reminded of the passage Isaiah 52: *"Depart, depart, go out from here there! Touch no unclean thing! Come out from it and be pure, you who carry the vessels of the Lord. But you will not leave in haste or go in flight; for the Lord will go before you, the God of Israel will be your rearguard."*

Inwardly, I had already separated having in some unidentified moment cut the cord between us. My course was set. The question of how I could actually leave remained unanswered for the moment. In the local Fellowship we had met one couple that became my friends. They were discerning, loving, and became aware of my problems long before I confided in them. A few days after our confidential talk, the wife arrived at the cottage with a gift. She knew I did not have money to travel with, nor the means to get from the village to the main railway station without involving Gordon, and she knew I was physically afraid of his anger. She pressed an envelope of money in to my hand, assuring me the gift came with her husband's blessing also. She said she would collect me and drive me to the railway station whenever I was ready. So the door swung open and all I had to do was go through it. Nevertheless, I had not yet been able to plan where to go, or how to live until I could get money to live on.

A family wedding invitation came to my aid. Afterwards I arranged to stay for a few days in Croydon with these relatives and Gordon readily agreed. We drove to the wedding together. I carried a small suitcase only and a spare key to the cottage.

I had won a small respite, but became keenly aware of another dilemma. How could I fully explain to his relatives, of whom I was fond, and who had always been most kind to me? I really needed a neutral place to plan my next move and after a nightmare-filled night, I contacted Grace's pastor and asked for his help. He arranged a room with a family in the church for which I was grateful. I arranged to move that evening. I had made my mind up not to tell my hosts about the real underlying problems. In part for fear of hurting them and because I just did not know how to put the whole sorry complex situation into words. But of course I hurt them anyway because I left without a full explanation, and they rightly felt used.

Once settled into the new household, I was offered a part-time job and, used to working, I accepted. In hindsight it might have been better to have rested and applied for Social Services financial aid, but anxious to establish as near to normal life as possible, I did not consider it. Before starting work, I managed to return to Salisbury where I was met and driven to the cottage by my friend. She had advised me Gordon was away and in about three hours, I was back on the train with all my own things and the spare key returned through the letterbox.

It was difficult then, phoning Gordon and explaining why I had done what I had in that manner. His rage was monumental, but at least I was at a little distance. Naturally, he was not prepared to accept my ultimatum or my reasons and harassed me a great deal. Through all this and getting to grips with a new job, I had not realized how great a strain I was under. I felt it, but had no way of knowing its effect. My hosts were kind, the pastor repeatedly asked me what I wanted to do, but suddenly I didn't know. The dammed up grief kept bursting through, and more than anything I needed time to settle.

Then several things combined to just add those last few straws to the camel's back, so to speak. I did not know quite what to do next. Instead of waiting until my over loaded emotions had settled down, I allowed myself to be pressurized into action. People round me were motivated by the best intentions, but the result was disastrous. My hostess took me along to consult a female divorce lawyer who was aggressive and not at all to my taste. I attempted to write a record of my reasons for wanting a divorce, but it brought me great stress, all before this line of action was really settled in my mind. I began to have nightmares and was further distressed by my hosts taking in another person in trouble, who was actually someone I had known in Africa. Seeing him so ill and in trouble and unable to even draw near for fellowship and friendship's sake (because of my hostess's instructions) left me saddened further. Then a particularly bad nightmare, more like a vision, of my husband stranded on a moonscape of rejection and loneliness threatened my fragile equilibrium.

On a journey one day, I tripped at the top of a flight of iron-edged steps in the railway station and severely injured my knee. It swelled alarmingly and my leg was soon twice its size for its full length. I was in considerable pain, not able to even bend my leg to sit properly. Insidiously, stress was building again.

Then came the day I became aware I was not functioning properly and was beginning to hallucinate but powerless to stop. I was taken to my hostess's doctor and later found myself left in a strange hospital, not even sure how I had got there. What I did not know, had never been told or warned about, was that the effects of the prescription drug Lorazapem (Ativan) stayed in one's system. After almost two years of nothing stronger than the occasional aspirin, I experienced a full-blown backlash of the withdrawal symptoms.

Within a few days I was moved to the rehabilitation ward, and allowed out on a shopping trip. I bought some beautiful dress material. I had been told I would go to a day-center for a further one week before being discharged.

Within an hour of arriving, before even getting to use the sewing facilities, an unknown culprit slashed my material to pieces. I was sent flowers, but another patient ripped them apart and threw them across the floor.

This was worse than anything I had experienced in the African hospital, and this whole second experience deeply shocked me. When I went for my frequent walks in the ground, I often saw an old decrepit 'bag-lady' hanging around the gate. She had all her possessions bundled into black plastic garbage bags on an old shopping trolley. She was dirty and no doubt homeless. I felt the enemy of my soul was taunting me and every walk became a spiritual battleground as I prayed and once more claimed my life back.

This time there was a new dimension to my fight for total healing and restoration. I had to continually fight back fear itself. Knowing that it was not of God, it nevertheless threatened to undermine my confidence. I had been told this sort of episode might happen again and I must be prepared to live accordingly, whatever that meant. Having previously been totally and joyously convinced of healing this knowledge was doubly hard, but I resolved not to take it on board.

God is faithful and true to his word. I latched on to scripture "greater is He who is in me, than the one who is in the world". I walked, prayed, and laid claim to all that was mine in the here and now: family, friends, health, ability to work and above all, a renewed spiritual ministry. And in direct response to the awful figure at the gate, I reminded myself and the enemy of who and what I really was: a daughter of The King, in neat clothes and good shoes, whose matching handbag held a check book and car keys. I was NOT going to live my life on the floor. This was no academic battle of words, this was my fight to affirm all the practical outworking of what I believed and the future I wanted.

Once discharged, after only matter of days, I stayed with Grace for a while, then used an apartment that became vacant next door to her for three weeks, but I still had to decide what to do. Despite my grip on renewal, it was harder this time to step out and make decisions. From time to time I suffered from depersonalization, a feeling of being unreal in my body. Sometimes I would be overcome with the fear that I could no longer do certain practical things and forced myself immediately to do that very thing, whatever it was; cooking, typing, sewing, crosswords, a scrabble game, accounts. I had to prove to myself that the fears were groundless.

Then there was the growing sense of homelessness. I took a temporary office job but the high tech equipment defeated me. The loss of my home, that source of quiet content, that pivotal core of my existence so hard won and joyfully shared, was painful indeed. The sense of being shut out and dispossessed overwhelmed me.

Back in Croydon, I found a temporary place with a family in the church and applied for Social Services aid. Without work and a proper place to stay, I was adrift and desperately tried to get into a stable situation. I moved to another friend's house and while I was there, my Canadian friend Mary came over to England on a brief visit. My hosts were kindness itself. Mary was a breath of fresh air, but the visit left me more sensitive to all I had lost, especially in the area of study and learning. I had neither the money, nor the strength as yet to go out and get what I instinctively knew I needed.

Chapter 24
Crutches

The need to establish a proper new life for myself continued to drive my outlook, but how to achieve it was another matter. Continual shortage of money severely limited my choices and I realized I could only reach my goals by taking very small steps.

When I began to look for a place of my own in earnest, I found city bed-sits with moldy walls and peeling paint acutely demoralizing and was quite unable to decide to rent one. I moved again, this time to a non-Christian house with four other lodgers, which was owned by a widow with a small child. As I was still in the Croydon district, I remained in fellowship at Grace's church. I did not want to be idle and realized the need to be busy, so instead of applying for Housing Benefit (Social Service financial aid for rent) I agreed to housekeep the whole house in return for my own room. In between times, I offered to do ironing for the pastor's household and other jobs, not allowing myself to watch TV until late in the day. Hal and Jo, now settled back in England, had given me a Television set and this was a great pleasure to me, but I disciplined myself and always worked in the mornings. Indeed, I did everything I could think of to regain confidence in my ability to function properly. At one point I became terrified I would lose my ability to remember things, so I gave myself exercises in recalling house numbers and street names whenever I walked to the shops.

The idea of going back to work was curiously daunting this late in life. No matter how much experience I had, how competent my former abilities, my recent experience had pulled the rug from underneath me, so to speak, in how I felt about myself. I had not been employed by anyone else for almost twenty years, in England for about thirty years. Employers only paid proper money for one to turn up and perform.

After three months, I applied to Social Services to pay my rent. I left off the housekeeping, and signed up for two courses at Croydon College; an introduction to Computers and Word Processing and 'Women in Management' in which there was little new for me basically, though it was valuable in the application of current conditions and information. I re-sat my UK driving test, which was no problem. My original driver's license had been lost in our house fire and being resident in Zambia with a Zambian license, I had no need to replace it before this. All this was enjoyable, and my confidence grew as my uncertainties diminished. But one area of my life remained unsettled.

The paper work regarding my proposed divorce lay in the drawer of the table in my room. From time to time that whole winter, I took it out, picked up my pen and put it away again. Though it only needed my signature to set the procedure rolling I could not bring myself to do it, and I knew deep down I had not fully accepted the fact that this was the only way out. Periodically, the whole problem would revolve in my mind, but no amount of reviewing the situation and trying to find another solution altered a thing.

Nor, it had to be said, was I ready to cope with the necessary upheaval of the divorce until I was in a more settled situation. It was as if, rebuilding my life step by step, I could not risk jeopardizing each small, hard-worn victory until I was sure the next effort would not over set what had gone before. I was determined I would never go through such a battle again and believed with all my heart God would help me to succeed. Also, I had no wish to involve or hurt my children further either by implication or the giving of details, if Gordon fought the case. I had learnt the hard way to distrust his reactions. It was already too late to apply for the divorce on grounds of adultery.

Despite the setbacks, the ill-advised counseling and my drawn out struggles, the church leadership had never wavered in their total support, even to one of them coming with me up to Birmingham to meet Gordon, who had found a job there. I had asked for a meeting on neutral ground to discuss a legal separation. He agreed to this though later reneged and refused to sign the legal papers.

However, now that I had come so far in re-establishing myself, and had become convinced a legal separation was the solution, I was content to wait and leave this for the moment. It was time to address the problem of finding work and a proper place to live, mindful that I had no pension or savings. There were still moves to make if I was to go after a professional job. For instance I needed a 'small job' to re-enter the workplace to gain confidence, and I had no suitable clothes. Also, even for a temporary period I did not want dingy accommodation and had no money for furnishing it anyway.

Accordingly, I decided to return to the Midlands, wondering if it were possible to prepare for this next step from my brother's home, where my mother also lived. The biggest problem was how long would it take me to achieve my goal.

With money, or the lack of it governing every practical decision, a strange opportunity presented itself and ever mindful of my ultimate goal, after prayer and thinking it through, I decided to accept it. I looked on it as a crutch to get me to the next place. Gordon wanted me to go back and I would not. However, we were able to have a discussion. I made it plain I would not resume a martial relationship and he informed me I would then have to pay my own expenses and half the household bills including pay for the telephone since I considered it a necessity.

I agreed and he took an additional room next to his on the ground floor of the house where he lodged. Installed in this temporary symbiotic relationship, I went job hunting. Thinking along the lines of some part-time office job, it was difficult until I became aware that there was a boy's boarding school in the same street advertising for a cook. Happily calling off my search for something bigger and better, I found in this something I could do more easily. In this job there was no need for smart clothes. There was a fair wage offered and the school only five minutes walk away. It enabled me to ease into the employer/employee and fellow worker roles again. After a few months, I was confident and began to think about the next step.

It was not easy being in such close proximity to Gordon again but no matter how odd it may have seemed to other people, or what he chose to tell them, the situation was clear from my point of view. He even agreed when a mutual friend urged him into some counseling and I supported him in this. But after a short time he pulled out. For those few winter months the truce held until events combined to push me forwards again.

One dark February morning I went to work as usual and shortly after breakfast was served, I tripped over a shallow unlighted step in the basement storerooms. The fall shook me but not until the agony struck a bit later did I realize I had sustained a bad injury. After several hours in the local hospital casualty ward I was sent home with a torn ligament in my hip. For the next nine weeks I could only hobble on crutches a short distance when the power of my painkiller tablets were at maximum strength.

Hardly settled into this new' painful and practically housebound routine, Gordon said he was off to Zambia for an unspecified time. Some time earlier I had discovered the farmhouse rents had not been paid for a considerable time, indeed the tenant had left the house vacant and the whole place sadly neglected. Attempting to open up the subject by asking Gordon why the tenant had not been accountable to him and his default thereby discovered sooner, I was told sharply, "it's none of your business" and for another six years I heard no further news of the farm.

My employers were not able to keep my job open beyond the end of the first month and I was not eligible for any sort of sick benefit. A telephone call in March to the Social Services resulted in me receiving incorrect information, so I had no further income until I was fit enough to go in person to apply. Then I had to wait another two weeks for the assistance to arrive. My one helper was a Christian student that lived in the same building. My student friend drove me to the hospital for treatments and another helped me by twice weekly shopping. Both these young women were a great blessing to me for which I was very thankful.

While I was trapped in my inactive routine within the apartment I delighted in watching the garden green up and the daffodils dance in the sun outside my windows. But in myself, strengthening changes were being forged, on one hand by waiting on the Lord and planning what I would do about getting a better job when I was fit, and on the other hand by the knowledge I gained in this period.

Gordon had obtained a job as student accommodation maintenance man at a college. He found friends and local fellowship and was already prominent in a house group. He had laid down a foundation of half-truths, which even after my arrival no one questioned. However, in the circumstances I was not directly involved or responsible and did not come to understand this fully until he was away.

In his absence however, I learned he had implied that I was permanently mentally unfit. A friend of his came to the house one day and when I answered the door and introduced myself, this person expressed surprise saying my husband had recently mentioned I was still in hospital. She would not leave a message and left abruptly.

Maybe he did it to get the 'sympathy' vote with the Christians there, or was it pride to put himself in a good light as a man on his own in their midst. Who can tell? It was all too complex for me to fathom. I had thought some of the folk at the college seemed a little wary of me but had dismissed that idea as fanciful. Now with this knowledge, my visceral reaction to him revived.

When he returned it was in the college Easter vacation. My injury was almost healed. However, he immediately announced he was going away again. Out of interest to see what he would say, I asked him if he could not delay a few days until after my birthday so we could go out since I had been housebound for so long. He said no, his trip could not wait and he would be off the following morning. So I knew that once again there would be no time to talk.

That night when he went for a bath before bed, I noticed his briefcase left open on the table. The rubber-stamped address on the top half of a large brown envelope was to be clearly seen above the pocket on the lid of the case. What drew my eye like a magnet was that it was the address of my doctor's office in Lusaka. Beginning to tremble I drew it out. It was bulky with my husband's name hand-written across the front. Without compunction and with a pounding heart I carefully steamed it open, all the while listening with bated breath for sounds from the bathroom along the hallway. There in my hand, I held my complete medical history in Zambia.

My mind grappled with the question, what was his motive in procuring such records? What was he planning to do with them? How had he managed to do that? With shaking hands I hastily found and wadded sheets of blank typing paper to approximate the same bulk and put them in the envelope, resealed it as best I could and replaced it in the briefcase. I hid the medical records under the carpet beneath the table. Then I called 'goodnight' in the direction of the still closed bathroom door and went to bed.

The next day after his departure, I called my support team, handed over the medical records for safekeeping and arranged for the team to come to the house upon my husband's return. Suddenly I was in the clear, calm and sure of myself. I knew what I should do. All doubts and uncertainties were laid to rest. The time had come to finish it. The day after his return, the support team came over and I was able at last to calmly explain my decision to leave immediately. Before one of the team drove me to my brother's house, we made arrangements for Gordon to be away from the house the next morning while I removed my things. He never challenged me about the missing medical records. Shortly after that the papers were burnt as a symbol of the past put behind me.

Chapter 25
Sufficient Grace

The heap of black plastic bags on my brother's garage floor was reminiscent of my earlier flights, but now it was different. It was not the end of anything it was the beginning. While my head grappled with practical problems, I could feel the sap rising in my heart and spirit.

Furnished with the best publication I could find for my purpose, I sat down and drew up a list on a large piece of paper. When I first arrived at my brother's house, I had thought to find a job, any job as quickly as possible, but after praying about it, I realized now was the time to go about the task more carefully. If I was going to expect to receive the fulfillment of those promises I believed were mine, I must do all I could to put myself in the way, in the path of that possibility. Accordingly, I drew up columns and listed what I needed, what I wanted, where I thought I should be, and why. Finally, alongside all of this, I wrote out the specific words I had received from God.

It had to be a good job that had enough salary to allow me to buy some pension, make a proper home and establish a new life. Instead of just going anywhere where I knew no one, it made good sense to be near one part of my family or another, which gave me three options: Solihull, Sussex or Croydon. With my checklist now complete I opened the publication and began to search the "situations vacant".

There was the job that had the potential to fulfill every condition on my list. Applications had to be within six days so I telephoned for an application form. I was told that the job had been advertised for some weeks, this being the last time. Then I went out to find a secretarial agency that could prepare me a professional resume. Later I telephoned the two most likely people available that could give me references. As soon as the form arrived, I carefully prepared my application and posted it back with out delay. On the afternoon of the day applications were closed, a telephone call from London invited me to report for an interview the following Thursday at 11.30am.

That evening I called Grace and arranged to sleep on her sofa the following Wednesday night, explaining why I wanted her to book me into her hairdresser early on the morning of the interview that was to be held not far away. We enjoyed a lovely visit while I pressed my one good dress and polished my shoes.

The interview was held in a small lounge off the dining room that sat eighty people. Though I had no formal qualifications, I had a wealth of practical experience and felt confident and calm. After the interview and conducted tour, I returned to Grace's flat to collect my overnight bag and set off for the railway station for the return trip to Solihull. Four hours later, as I entered my brother's house, my sister-in-law met me in the hall with the news that she had received a telephone message: the job was mine. Getting the job was not only a great relief, there was also a very nice unfurnished apartment that went with it, which was newly decorated and carpeted. Stuart, who had returned from America a short time before, was in the next suburb and Grace even nearer.

When the euphoria had settled a little, I began to think of what I must do next. There was barely two weeks to go before taking up my appointment and I had almost no money. But reluctant to borrow from my family, I prayerfully made out yet another list of the very least of my needs, including the matter of the move itself. Stuart hired a self-drive van on my behalf and drove my things down to my new place the following weekend.

My mother gave me an old but comfortable easy chair and a TV set round which we packed my bags, a few basic dishes and so on. But I had only one good dress and pair of shoes that I had worn to the interview and a good wool coat, a gift from my family. Everything else had come from charity shops and was too well worn to be suitable for my new situation.

Once more I went to prayer holding the paper on which I had written my promises side by side my needs, only this time they were clipped to my job confirmation letter. The next day I went across town to the Bank I had used while working and where I had left $15 just to keep the account open. After prayer I had telephoned ahead to ask for an appointment with the manager.

Seated across from the lady Assistant Bank Manager, I produced my letter of appointment that stated my salary. Feeling steady now with a real sense of peace, I briefly explained my position, saying I needed to get a bed, and an iron, together with a few more clothes and to be able to keep myself until my first paycheck. I then asked for a $500 overdraft. She said, "Yes, I think we can do that for you." So after a few formalities I was out in the street again in a very short space of time, feeling very relieved and thankful.

My particular appointment, in the block of eighty-two apartments for retired teachers, was that of Deputy Warden over sixty-two "sheltered" apartments for the elderly, including the responsibility for catering. I took my main meal on duty and that helped enormously that first month. Grace came round with an ironing board so after the first week I did not have to iron my clothes on the floor. Soon I was able to add basic furniture piece by piece and slowly my new life began.

181

Divorce. It was bereavement without dignity, a form of death without a body and a burial. No matter that the world found it commonplace, it grieved me deeply. In it, there exists a strange dichotomy for a Christian. There is no hiding it and it signals some degree of failure, subtly altering other people's perception of one. In the end it happened very quietly, a mere exchange of documents between lawyers, ironically becoming final on Grace's birthday.

Holding my divorce papers I wept again, grieving that I had been pushed into such a position. My husband had sworn he would see I never got a penny if I went through with it. With all his property in Zambia, I knew it was futile to try. All I wanted, as I promised myself when I left Africa, was to find a way to bring about, to create something good from my time there. When I came away there were no fond farewells, no accolades or good wishes from friends or colleagues, just a lonely exit shadowed in shame.

At that time, in such dark circumstances, I had difficulty remembering any of the good stuff. With so many reasons to put the past behind me, I was nevertheless reluctant to the see the 'baby' thrown out with the bath water. The 'baby' in this case being all the good and lovely things I had experienced from the hand of God, the joys and precious times I could rightly praise and thank Him for, the hopes and dreams I had entrusted to Him.

Before I left Africa and for a long time after my return to England, I was engaged in the humbling process of evaluating my past choices and decisions, but I remained unshaken in the conviction that my long fight had been worthwhile. Learning the hard way, that no amount of love, devotion, loyalty, faith or prayer will move a man against his unrepentant will, was a devastating lesson. But however naïve and mistaken I may be judged, I did not regret my choice to stay so long. What does the marriage service say? *"...to love and to cherish...forsaking all others...for better or worse....till death do us part."* Love had died a hard, lingering death while I tried to fulfill my half of the contract.

I had long accepted my struggles and disappointment in the marriage knowing well how imperfect I was also, but adultery was a far cry from all I learned much later. The knowledge that a greater, more damaging betrayal was the crux of the matter, and I had been powerless to prevent it, was my most bitter burden.

Yet how faithful is our God, how swift to reach out and restore us once we turn to him. How patient and ready He is to teach us how to rebuild. I would not trade past anguish for what I learned of His grace.

Sometime in my childhood, my mother have me a book and she wrote on the flyleaf: *"This above all: to thine own self be true, and it must follow as the night the day thou canst not then be false to any man."* William

Shakespeare Hamlet Act 1, scene 3.

How often these words had echoed in my mind over the years more especially as I had struggled to find my way through the mire of deceit to become my own person once again.

What had God promised me? In 1984 at the height of my tribulations He spoke into my situation through godly counselors. The assurance that I was understood and the encouragement I found in the knowledge of the scriptures gave me a solid base from which to rise. Although this Calvary journey had taken time, it produced a far deeper understanding and a wider, more objective view of an era and a family, a purpose and its trials, and above all, the encompassing, never failing strength of God's redeeming love.

Looking back over the way God had led, where I struggled and fought, sacrificed and at last capitulated, there is no instance where He left me. After our fire that took all our material goods, only a tiny portion of brick wall was left standing undamaged. It is a mute testimony to *"The Lord is good, a stronghold in the day of trouble: and He knows them that trust in Him."* Nahum 1: 7

I learned that whatever my circumstances I could count on Him for all I needed in everything I was going through. When the spirit of discouragement threatened to drag me down, and the enemy whispered *'You're not going to make it'*, He gave me the courage I needed. God has never said anything He could not back up. He never promised anything He could not deliver. Though some answers took time, He was there in the waiting room. That is God's grace. And it is possible to go forward in peace and hope knowing the best is yet to come.

End

Glossary

Amoyo	life
Amayi	mother, older woman
Bambo	old gentleman (respectful)
Bilharzias	An African waterborne disease.
Bwana	Boss
Bwerani	come (command)
Bwerani kuno	come here
Chibuku	native beer made from maize
Chabwino	It is good.
Chitenge	A length of cotton dress goods.
Dambo	open damp grassy area, swamp
Kanyoni	small birds of the bush
Kapenta	tiny lake fish
Khasu	garden hoe
Khaya	hut, shed
Katundu	luggage, baggage
Kuyenda	to walk, to travel
Kyinu?	"and you?"
Kusanga	go to the bush
Manzi	water
Matete	reeds
Mipando	chair, stool
Ndeke	airplane
Ndiri bwino	"I am well."
Njoka	snake
Nshima	stiff maize porridge, staple food

Odi	"excuse me"
Phiri	hill
Relish	tomato based vegetable mixture
Rondavel	typical African roundhouse
Tengani	bring (command)
Tiyende	let's go
Tiyenda ku caya bala	"go with the ball"="let's play football"
Zikomo	thank you
Zirombo	weeds

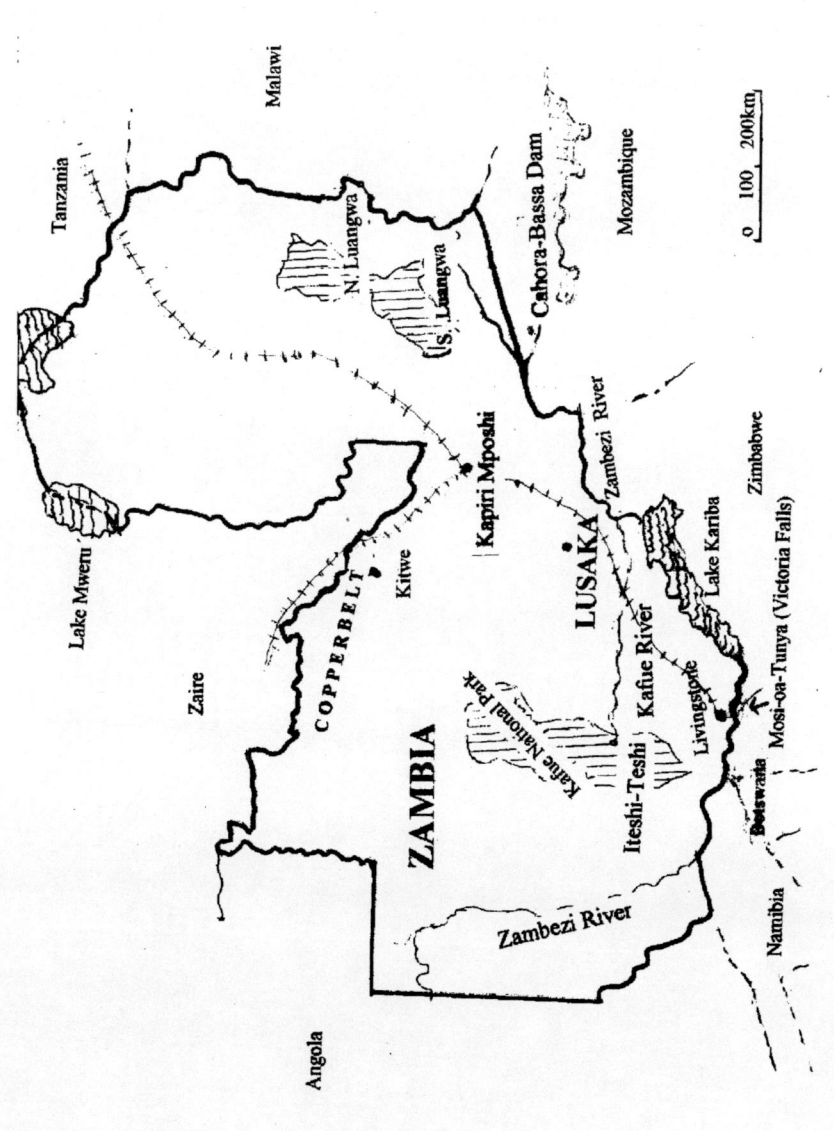